ENGLISH 101

FIRST-YEAR COMPOSITION

Third Edition

**Marcy Taylor, Elizabeth Brockman, and Melinda Kreth
with Laura Grow**

*Department of English Language and Literature
Central Michigan University*

KENDALL/HUNT PUBLISHING COMPANY
4050 Westmark Drive   Dubuque, Iowa   52002

TABLE OF CONTENTS

Introduction to ENG 101: First-Year Composition

Chapter 1: Writing Processes and Purposes

Chapter 2: Reading & Responding to Texts

Chapter 3: Rhetorical Analysis

Chapter 4: Writing from Multiple Sources

Chapter 5: Reflecting on Your Literacy

Chapter 6: Essays for Analysis

Introduction to ENG 101: First-Year Composition

First-Year Composition at CMU

English 101 is a first-year writing course that fulfills part of the Written Competency Requirement, an important element of CMU's General Education Program. Because writing is linked to success in college and in the professional world, CMU requires two semesters of composition plus writing-intensive courses throughout the University Program.

English 101 is designed to help students develop their writing skills, not only in terms of academic writing, but also in terms of a basic understanding of composing processes and grammatical correctness so that students can function successfully in diverse writing situations in and beyond college. Below are the objectives of the course, as presented in the master syllabus. Although the actual assignments and schedules may vary slightly, every section of English 101 strives to help students achieve these objectives.

Course Objectives from the ENG 101 Master Syllabus

General Course Objective:
The development of increasingly skilled writing is the focus of English 101. The course provides intensive practice in the intellectual and verbal habits required by a wide variety of public writing, including careful reading, critical thinking, and coherent writing.

Specific Objectives:
Composing Processes: By the end of English 101, students should be able to
- understand that writing is a recursive process that usually requires multiple drafts;
- understand that writing is a means of discovery as well as a means of communication and be able to use writing for both purposes;
- develop flexible strategies for generating, revising, editing, and proofreading;
- understand and be able to responsibly perform collaborative aspects of writing processes, including critiquing their own and others' works and implementing advice from the instructor and others; and
- use computer word-processing operations and other technologies to research, compose, revise, edit, and format papers.

Rhetorical Knowledge: By the end of English 101, students should be able to
- understand that effective writers need knowledge of topics, genres, and rhetorical strategies;
- recognize that texts have rhetorical purposes and that successful writers negotiate the rhetorical demands of differing discourse communities;
- write texts that define, restrict, and illustrate topics;
- form and evaluate effective theses or claims;
- evaluate and use a variety of different principles of organization in paragraphs and texts;
- adjust tone, diction, and content to different audiences; and
- find, evaluate, analyze, and integrate with their own thinking appropriate primary and secondary sources (e.g., textual, visual, and auditory sources) and understand when such sources are necessary to a successful written text.

> **Knowledge of Conventions:** By the end of English 101, students should be able to
> - understand the conventions associated with different genres, including the use of common formats of different kinds of texts;
> - be aware of the features of standard written English, especially those that distinguish it from spoken English;
> - write prose without clichés, verbosity, and monotonous syntax;
> - write prose in standard written English free of errors that undermine the writer's credibility, such as comma mistakes, spelling errors, and errors in agreement; and
> - document sources correctly.

Notice that the objectives are divided into three overlapping areas: composing processes, rhetorical knowledge, and knowledge of conventions. Each assignment sequence in the course will include all three areas. In other words, with each assignment you will practice strategies for planning, drafting, and revising your papers, as well as responding to other students' texts; you will explore various rhetorical techniques and issues, including understanding audiences and purposes for writing; and you will work to edit your work and to learn conventions of grammar, mechanics, and style that you have not mastered yet.

This textbook will provide much, although not all, of the information you will need to successfully meet the course objectives related to composing processes and rhetorical knowledge. You will need additional resources to meet the course objectives related to knowledge of conventions, which is why your instructor has probably also required you to purchase a handbook of some sort that includes valuable information on grammar, punctuation, usage, source citation, and so forth. Many ENG 101 instructors also required students to purchase *They Say, I Say* by Gerald Graff and Cathy Birkenstein, which is a handy little book designed to help you learn how to summarize, paraphrase, and quote sources, as well as how to effectively incorporate information from sources into your own writing (a skill that you will focus on in Assignment 3: The Bibliographic Essay). In addition to your textbooks, your instructor may also place on Blackboard or at the Park Library other documents and resources relevant to the class.

In addition to the textbooks and other materials made available to you, your instructor will structure the course to include a variety of learning opportunities. Sometimes your instructor will need to deliver "mini-lectures" to provide you with information or explain various aspects of an assignment, but most of your class time will be spent

- discussing assigned readings and sample essays from this textbook, from other sources, and/or from among students in the class (anonymously, of course)
- reviewing completed homework and in-class assignments
- completing practice activities (e.g. punctuation practice, citation practice)
- completing in-class writings (both informal and formal)
- participating in peer revision workshops
- viewing relevant videos for analysis and discussion

There will be plenty of time in class for you to ask questions about anything you don't understand. You can also email questions to your instructor or drop by during his or her scheduled office hours.

Be sure to carefully read your instructor's syllabus, and make sure you understand his or her policies on attendance, late assignments, revisions, academic integrity, and so forth. You won't be able to later claim ignorance as an excuse for not doing what you're supposed to do.

Grading Criteria

Students must receive a "C" (not a "C-") to receive competency credit for ENG 101. The grading criteria for all major writing assignments and in-class writings are linked to the course objectives. These are standards that reinforce the outcomes for the course, and they are consistent across all sections of English 101. It is important that you understand these criteria so that you can write quality essays that adequately respond to them.

Responsiveness

A paper should respond to the specific terms of the assignment. In other words, if you're asked to write a rhetorical analysis and you write a personal reflection, you will not receive credit for the assignment. Also, any revision of the paper should demonstrate that you have considered your peers' and teacher's comments, as well as the description of the other grading criteria below. A paper that fails to meet all the terms of the assignment will not receive a passing grade, regardless of whatever other positive features it might exhibit.

Purpose

A paper should be organized around a clear conceptual center or thesis, i.e. a reason for you to be writing and for your reader to be reading. Your thesis should clearly and concisely articulate one point or arguable claim, something neither trivial nor self-evident.

Organization/Unity

A well-organized paper develops logically. Each point builds on the one before it. The paper should include transitions within and between paragraphs to let the reader know where the essay is going and how the parts of the paper are connected. Readers don't appreciate papers that seem like connect-the-dots pictures before the dots have been connected. As the writer, it's your job to connect the dots. Appropriate emphasis should be placed on each part of the paper so that central ideas receive more attention and minor ones receive less. A unified paper excludes padding, digression, and anything else that is not relevant to the thesis; every paragraph should have a purpose, and every sentence should help construct the meaning of the paragraph and support the overall argument. Most paragraphs will need to begin with clear, well-focused topic sentences that indicate to readers what the paragraph is about.

Support/Development

A well-developed paper is thorough enough to satisfy a skeptical reader. Descriptions should be detailed enough for readers to see, hear, and otherwise experience the event, place, or situation being described. Explanations should be clear and sufficiently detailed. Evidence presented should be appropriate for your intended audience and purpose.

Presentation

Writing with authority requires effective presentation and style. If your instructor has stipulated a particular format for your paper, be sure to follow the instructions. If not, then consider what format will be most effective for the paper. Would headings be helpful to readers? Are sources cited using correct documentation format? A paper that includes spelling or grammatical errors, unclear sentences, inappropriate diction, half-formed ideas, or digressions will do little to give the reader confidence in you or your work.

Other Course-related Issues

In your instructor's syllabus, he or she has included policies about attendance, plagiarism, late assignments, missed revision workshops, what counts as "substantive" revision, make-ups of in-class writings, and so on. It's your responsibility to read and understand these policies, just as it's your responsibility to read and understand *all* CMU policies and procedures.

Throughout the semester, keep an eye on the withdrawal dates. Your instructor may decide to submit web-based attendance reports to the Registrar's office but is not required to do so. These reports are intended to track students who may be "at risk," as well as those who may be fraudulently obtaining student loans for classes they are not attending. If you receive an attendance notice from the Registrar's office, then either start attending class and doing the course work or withdraw from the course to avoid receiving a failing grade.

If you have a question or concern about your grade on an assignment or in the course, you must follow the "chain of command," so to speak. You should begin by scheduling an appointment with your instructor to calmly and rationally discuss the issue. The key words here are "calmly and rationally." That means that you should present yourself reasonably, not emotionally: don't accuse, harangue, harass, scream, cry, or in any other way display immature, disrespectful, or unprofessional behavior—doing so will undermine your credibility. Approaching the situation rationally won't *guarantee* that you'll get what you want, but it's much more likely using this approach than any others.

If, after you have met with your instructor, you still feel your concern has not been adequately addressed, then you may arrange a meeting with the Director of Composition. Most problems are resolved at this level; however, if yours is not, you may then contact the Chair of the English Department. Do *not* try to "go around" your instructor or the Director of Composition and appeal directly to the Chair, because the Chair will not meet with you until you have first met with your instructor and the Director of Composition.

The CMU Writing Center

One of the best resources CMU offers to *all* students, not just composition students, is the CMU Writing Center. According to the Writing Center Director, Dr. Mary Ann Crawford, "The CMU Writing Center is dedicated to supporting a culture of writing in the University community and to providing a collaborative environment that assists writers in developing writing strategies and skills across disciplines and beyond."

The Writing Center offers a variety of services for students: on-site consulting for all students and an online service offered to ENG 101 students and all students in CMU's Off-Campus programs. If you need help with prewriting, drafting, revising, editing, or polishing, visit the Writing Center.

If you and your 101 instructor agree that you have strong writing skills and you think you might be interested in working as a consultant at the Writing Center, contact Dr. Mary Ann Crawford at crawf1ma@cmich.edu or 989-774-2986.

Writing Center staff include paid and for-credit peer writing consultants, several graduate assistants, a director, and two associate directors. In their first semester of working at the Center, all consultants participate in ENG 510, the Writing Center Practicum class, whether for credit and/or for pay, usually with a combination of the two. Ongoing training continues during staff meeting and as needed for individual consultants throughout the year. Also associated with the Writing Center is a registered student organization, the Writing Circle, which invites all university students to participate in writing and teaching writing activities and which allows members to apply for funds to support programs as well as conference travel.

On-Campus Services

- **Park Library 400** (northwest corner of the 4th floor)
  Mon. - Thurs., 9 a.m. - 9 p.m.
  Sun., 6 p.m. - 9 p.m.
  989-774-2986
- **Anspach 003**
  Mon. - Thurs., 9 a.m. - 4 p.m.
  Fri., 9 a.m. - 1 p.m.
  989-774-1228
- **The Towers** (Wheeler Hall basement)
  Mon. - Thurs., 1 p.m. - 4 p.m. and 6 p.m. - 9 p.m.
  989-774-1002
- **IAC** (athletes only)
  Sun. - Thurs., 7 p.m. - 9 p.m.

Off-Campus Services

Online service is available for students enrolled in ENG 101 and in Off-Campus Programs courses. For questions about this service, email writcent@cmich.edu or call 989-774-2986.

Chapter 1: Writing Processes and Purposes

Writing Processes

Perhaps you have learned in your previous schooling that writing is a *process;* this is not a new idea. And you probably know that, in most cases, writers go through steps of prewriting (e.g. gathering information, brainstorming, outlining, etc.), drafting, getting feedback, revising, and proofreading and editing. Figure 1 illustrates this process, showing also that the process can be—and often is—repeated (i.e. it's recursive). However, writing processes vary from writer to writer and from one writing situation to the next. For example, the writer of a workplace memo might complete some or all of the steps quite quickly, whereas the writer of a scholarly research article or a novel will probably go through the process many times, over a much longer period. As author and editor E. B. White was fond of reminding writers, "the best writing is rewriting."

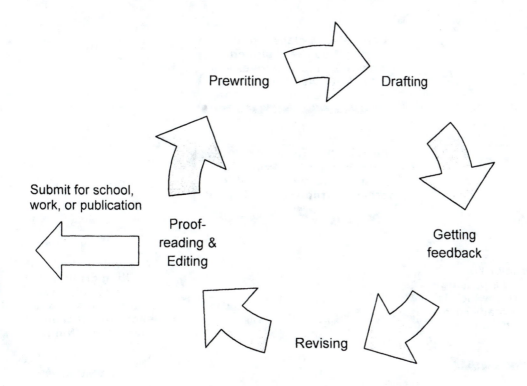

Figure 1: A recursive writing process

Focusing on writing processes in this course will help you explore and develop *strategies* for composing that will be the most productive for you, adding to your repertoire of techniques and honing your skills so that writing becomes more fluent and automatic.

Many new college students rely on ineffective writing processes. Figure 2 illustrates one such process; perhaps you or someone you know has relied on this process. In contrast, Figure 3 illustrates an effective writing process; it reflects various tasks that need to be completed for the writer to reasonably expect an effective outcome.

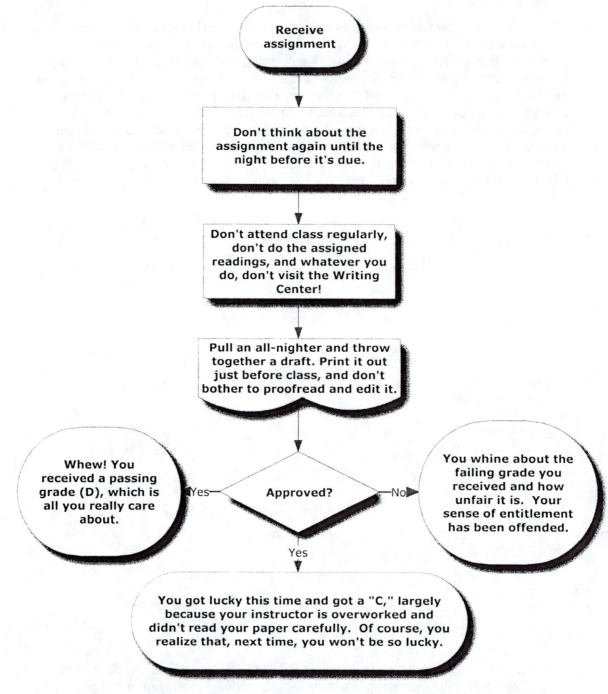

Figure 2: An ineffective writing process

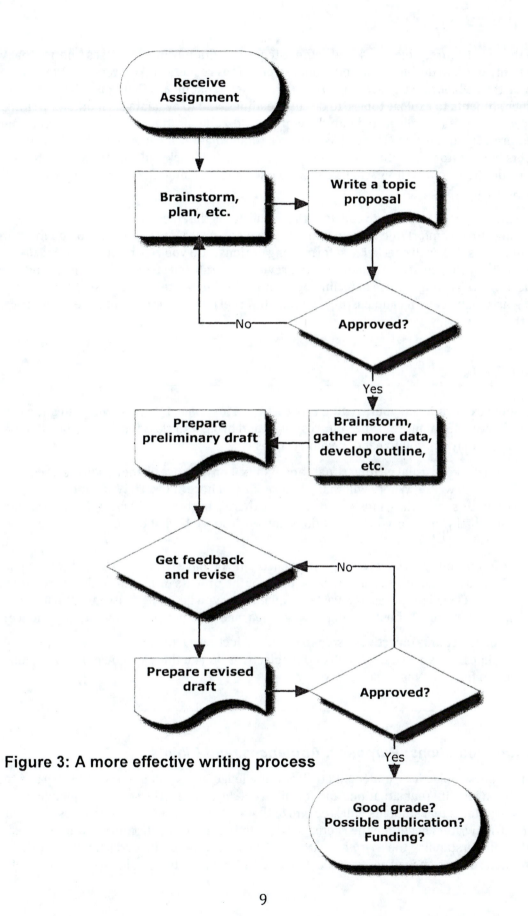

Figure 3: A more effective writing process

9

In the list of course objectives, under the category of "Composing Processes," notice that we not only work to develop your individual strengths as readers and writers, but we also value the collaborative aspects of writing processes. That means that you will work with other students to explore topics, to discuss readings, and to evaluate each other's writing. As you progress in college and into the work world, collaboration will become increasingly required and important. None of us writes in total isolation; even professional novelists and poets have editors and others on whom they rely for feedback and constructive criticism. Consider how your writing rituals and processes might be modified in positive ways by the presence of others.

The final aspect of process to consider this semester is the role of technology in your writing. How comfortable are you with using a word-processor to write? Do you make use of functions like spell checker and formatting options? Do you rely on them *too much?* What about sharing texts with others and reviewing drafts electronically? These and other questions regarding the use of technology (and the *misuse* of technology, such as plagiarizing by copying and pasting from the Internet) will be important aspects of process in this course.

Exercise 1

Do some exploration of your writing processes. Choose *one* of the following questions and write for 30–45 minutes. Type your response and bring it to class for discussion. Your instructor may ask you to hand in your responses.

A. Describe your usual writing rituals and habits. For instance, is there a preferred *place* for you to write? Where will that place be for you here at CMU? What about *tools*, like computers, materials, music, and so on? Is there a best time of day? Why do you think that ritual works for you (or, if it does not work so well, what do you need to do differently)?

B. Describe your previous writing experiences. If you have trouble writing, try to explain why it is difficult for you and what aspects of the process or mental activity are difficult. If you feel well prepared as a writer, explain how you got to be that way. What important "rules" about writing have you learned through your previous experience?

C. Using the course objectives listed in the Introduction, write about your strengths and weaknesses as a writer. Which of the objectives do you think will be most important for you to focus on this semester? Why?

Writing Situations: Purposes, Audiences, and Claims

In the course objectives, under "Rhetorical Knowledge," we want students to learn strategies for writing in different situations and for different audiences. The second objective in that category states that students will "recognize that texts have rhetorical purposes and that successful writers negotiate the rhetorical demands of differing discourse communities." This means understanding the *writing situation.* A writing situation involves the writer, the intended readers, the purposes of the text, and the eventual text itself. Notice that all of these elements are changeable; that's why a writer has to be flexible enough to *negotiate* the situations by changing strategies. There is no "good writing" that is effective in every situation with every audience. That is why in this course, and in ENG 201, we stress writing for a variety of purposes, in a variety of genres, and for a variety of audiences.

Purposes

The purpose of a piece of writing determines the form and content of the piece, so it is crucial to understand what *effect* you want to have on an audience. Sometimes your instructors—and later, your employers, clients, customers, and so on—will assign your purposes, in which case you have to understand what they want you to produce and why; other times, you will have more choice. Sometimes you will write just to *express* yourself or to *learn* something through writing notes or journal entries. (We call these *writer-based purposes.*) On the other hand, even though all writing is to some degree personal, we often write to communicate with others. When we write to *explain, define, persuade, analyze, demonstrate understanding,* or *entertain,* we are writing for *audience-* or *subject-based purposes.* Sometimes our writing can serve multiple purposes and reach multiple audiences.

Audiences

Stephen Reid, in *The Prentice Hall Guide for College Writers,* suggests asking the following questions about your audience to help you plan a piece of writing:

- How much information or evidence is enough? What should I assume my audience already knows? What should I not tell them? What do they believe? Will they readily agree with me, or will they be antagonistic?

- How should I organize my writing? How can I get my readers' attention? Can I just describe my subject and tell a story, or should I analyze everything in a logical order? Should I put my best examples or arguments first or last?

- Should I write informally, with simple sentences and easy vocabulary, or should I write in a more elaborate or specialized style, with technical vocabulary? (24)

You can see that by analyzing your audience, you answer questions that determine how you research and shape your writing. It is also possible, however, that your sense of audience will become clearer as you write. That is, you may envision or *construct* an audience as you write. This is especially true when writing for a generic or unknown audience, such as when writing an assignment for a class (like this one).

Claim or Thesis

The *claim,* or *thesis,* of a piece of writing is the dominant idea or main point, and it is related to purpose and audience. Obviously, your purpose (i.e. the effect you wish to have) will determine your thesis; as you gather information and shape your piece, you will narrow your idea until you have one main argument or idea to express. A thesis is narrower than a topic or a purpose; it expresses a claim that the writer then goes on to explore and develop. Your claim may be a claim of fact (i.e. that such-and-such is the case), a claim of value (i.e. that such-and-such is good or valuable or ethical), or a claim of policy (i.e. that we should do such-and-such). Claims of policy are supported by claims of fact and value, which are, in turn, supported by good evidence.

According to Diana Hacker, the author of the *Pocket Style Manual,* "thesis statements take a stand on a debatable issue—an issue about which intelligent, well-meaning people might disagree" (114). Knowing who your audience is and what its expectations might be will help you develop an arguable and effective thesis. That is how the elements of the writing situation—writer, purpose, audience, and thesis—are intimately related.

Exercise 2

Let's look at two short essays in terms of purpose, audience, and thesis. Read the essays in Chapter 6 by Robert Zoellner and Amy Tan, and then respond in writing to the following questions. Be prepared to share your responses in class. Your instructor may ask you to hand in your responses.

A. Which of the two essays did you find more interesting to read? Why? Which do you think is more "well written"? Why?

B. What is the *purpose* and *thesis* of each essay? (Cite specific parts of the texts as evidence to support your response.)

C. Zoellner's essay first appeared in a newspaper, *The Coloradoan;* Tan's essay appeared in *Life* magazine. Imagine the audiences for each of these pieces. Pick one of the essays, and describe what you think the audience is like, based on the way the author has written the piece. What do you think each author assumed about his or her audience?

D. Analyze the writing style of each essay for a minute. How would you describe the overall *tone* of each piece? The pieces are both personal essays; yet, they are quite different, and the writer's *voice* is one difference. Use evidence from the essays to describe the voice or tone the writer projects. Then evaluate: Which of the essays projects a more effective tone, given the audience and purpose?

Reading Strategies and the Composition Classroom[1]

Most of us have a bad attitude when it comes to reading assigned in school. Often, if we even bother to pick up the books at all, we move our eyes over the page and barely comprehend (and certainly do not retain) the information. When we're faced with challenging material, the problem is amplified. Ironically, our success in a course may

[1] We drew inspiration from the following sources in writing this section: Douglas Downs's "Rethinking Dogma: Teaching Critical Thinking in Freshman Composition" (Milwaukee: National Council of Teachers of English, 2000); Stephen Krashen's *The Power of Reading: Insights from the Research* (Englewood, CO: Libraries Unlimited, Inc., 1993); and Cris Tovani's *I Read It, But I Don't Get It: Comprehension Strategies for Adolescent Readers* (Portland, ME: Stenhouse Publishing, 2000).

depend in large part on our understanding of assigned reading, but we often lack the commitment and skills necessary to *engage* with the text.

In college, the way we are expected to read changes from the way most of us were expected to read in high school, but seldom does anyone bother to tell us that explicitly. Also, the *kinds* of texts we're expected to read in college are different from the kinds of texts most of us read in high school. In high school, we were accustomed to mining textbooks for facts for answering questions, or reading novels and short stories so that we could answer questions about plot, characters, and themes.

But college-level work requires a more *critical* approach, and you will often be expected to read more than just textbooks or works of fiction. You will also be expected to

- recognize that texts represent an author's perspective or point of view

- learn how to recognize the techniques authors use to build credibility and persuade effectively and how to use those techniques in your own writing

- see how texts fit together, as well as how they fit into our existing store of knowledge, in order to make connections between seemingly disparate ideas

- use those connections to help shape and support your own ideas

- learn how to do all those things on your own. The ability to adapt to this higher level of critical thinking and reading is often what separates college graduates from people who do not complete their education.

Much of the writing required in ENG 101, and in many of your other college classes, is based on reading and responding critically to texts. What follows are some tools that will make that critical reading easier.

Making Connections

A big part of understanding and retaining reading is being able to fit the new information into your existing knowledge. This is called *schema theory*, which is explained well in the following excerpt from Sharon Alayne Widmayer, a professor at George Mason University:

> All human beings possess categorical rules or scripts that they use to interpret the world. New information is processed according to how it fits into these rules, called schema. These schema can be used not only to interpret but also to predict situations occurring in our environment. Think, for example, of a situation where you were able to finish another person's thoughts, or when someone asked you to pass that "thingamabob." Schema Theorists suggest that you used your schema to predict what your conversation partner was going to say and to correctly interpret "thingamabob" as the hammer needed to nail something into the wall.

> Information that does not fit into these schema may not be comprehended, or may not be comprehended correctly. This is the reason why readers have a difficult time comprehending a text on a subject they are not familiar with even if the person comprehends the meaning of the individual words in the passage. If the waiter in a restaurant, for example, asked you if you would prefer to sing, you may have a difficult time interpreting what he was asking

13

and why, since singing is not something that patrons in a restaurant normally do. However, if you had been to the restaurant in the past and knew that it was frequented by opera students who liked to entertain the crowds, you would have incorporated that information into your schema and not [been] confused when the waiter asked if you'd prefer to sing.

[...] the learner in schema theory actively builds schema and revises them in light of new information. Each individual's schema is unique and depends on that individual's experiences and cognitive processes.

Critical reading is active reading. Often when you read, you make connections to your existing schemata on a barely conscious level. If a character in a story you are reading is tall, thin, and balding, you might picture him as looking like your tall, thin, balding uncle. When you read about soldiers fighting overseas, you might recall learning about World War II or Vietnam in history class. If you become more consciously aware of the connections you are making, this will help your reading comprehension in two ways. First, it will help you stay focused. It is very easy to drift away in the middle of what you are reading, but if you are looking for those connections as you read, you will stay better engaged with the text. Second, making connections will help you retain what you read. When you make connections between new and old information, what you read becomes part of your schema, a permanent part of how you view and understand the world. This is what we mean by *learning*, which you can see is very different from merely memorizing.

You can divide your connections to a text into two types: personal experience and academic connections. Sometimes the lines between these two blur, but there is a basic difference between knowledge you have acquired directly through your experiences and interactions outside of an academic setting and knowledge you have gained in a classroom. Depending on what you are reading, you may make many personal experience connections and no academic connections, or vice versa.

It helps to be aware of what kind of connections you are making so that you better understand how you process and comprehend new information. Is your schema based more on personal experience, or has your academic training been more influential? Are there certain topics in which you only have one kind of connection or the other? Being more aware of your answers to these questions will help you with the second reading comprehension strategy, *questioning*.

Asking Questions

You will almost never read something that leaves you with no questions. Whether it is something as simple as "What does that word mean?" or as big as "What is the author's main point?" if you are engaged with what you are reading, you should be asking and answering your own questions. One might divide the types of questions people ask into two categories: knowledge questions and global questions.

Knowledge Questions

No one knows everything, and the further you advance in your college education, the more you will encounter texts that are difficult to understand, because they use words, make references, and discuss concepts with which you are not familiar. This means you have a gap in knowledge that prevents you from comprehending the text; in other words, you don't have a schema into which to fit this new information. *The single worst mistake you can make as a reader is not to fill that gap in knowledge so you can understand the text.*

Lazy readers skip words they don't know, ignore unfamiliar references, and pass over passages about new concepts (and in college, laziness usually translates into poor grades; after college, it could cost you a job or ruin your business). Sometimes this "lazy" strategy works, because context clues from other parts of the text can shed light on confusing sections. However, if those clues don't help, it is imperative that you turn to outside resources to answer your questions. These are called *knowledge questions,* because all it takes is a little extra knowledge to answer them. If you don't look up the word you don't know, then you'll never know if it's a word that's important for understanding the author's meaning. If you don't look up references, you won't know if they are key to understanding, for example, a particularly important comparison or contrast. If you don't look to outside sources for explanations of confusing concepts, you will miss key parts to a text.

In short, you can never be sure you actually comprehend a text unless you answer your own questions and fill in those knowledge gaps. This does not have to be difficult. A dictionary and the Internet are probably the only two things you need to get a good enough answer to allow you to reread a confusing section of a text and make sense of it.

Global Questions

Global questions are entirely different from knowledge questions, because global questions do not have right or wrong answers. *Global questions* are the kinds of questions that arise from contemplating the issues brought up in a text. One way to think about the difference is that, usually, knowledge questions would ask *who, what, when, where,* or *how,* but global questions would ask *why?* Common types of global questions are about contemporary social issues (Should gay people be allowed to marry?), human nature (Why do people treat waitresses and other service industry workers poorly?), and values (Is it wrong to steal food if you are starving?).

Global questions are equally as important as knowledge questions, because whereas knowledge questions allow you to understand a text, global questions open up the possibility for you to go beyond the text and to think and write about your own ideas and the ideas of other people. Once again, according to Diana Hacker, the author of the *Pocket Style Manual*, "thesis statements take a stand on a debatable issue—an issue about which intelligent, well-meaning people might disagree" (114). Because all academic writing, and much workplace writing, is based on some type of thesis, it is important that you be able to identify "issue[s] about which intelligent, well-meaning people might disagree." In other words, you need to be able to recognize global questions in what you read, because those global questions should provide the groundwork or inspiration for your own writing.

Annotation: Bridging the Gap between the Mind and the Page

The root word of *annotation* is *note.* There is no one right way to annotate a text when you read, but annotating is not just highlighting or underlining as you read. Highlighters are a perfectly acceptable annotation tool, but annotating involves much more engagement with the text and much more thinking. Annotation is taking notes as you read, either on the text itself (e.g. in the margins, but never in a book or other publication you don't own—make a copy first) or on a separate piece of paper (or sometimes both). As you annotate, you should be highlighting or underlining parts of the text that you think are important. (Hint: To avoid overhighlighting, target only words and phrases, not whole sentences, or target individual sentences, not whole paragraphs.) But you should also be writing down your personal experience and academic connections, as well as your knowledge questions and global questions.

If you are reading a series of texts that revolve around the same theme or topic (as you will later for Assignment 3), you should write down specific connections (comparisons and contrasts) among the texts. Another invaluable annotation process would be to write short, simple summaries of the material in your own words (even in the margins) so that you can keep track of what the author is talking about and also find information more easily when you have to refer to the text later. Annotation is important, because even though you might be doing all the comprehension strategies in your head as you read, taking the time to write them down preserves your connections and questions for future contemplation, and the act of writing improves your chances of retaining the information.

Some Reading Hints

- Never skip prefaces, introductions, or conclusions. They usually contain a wealth of clues as to what the text is about. Reading these before you tackle a text will help you develop a schema into which to fit the rest of the text.

- If possible, find out a little about the author or authors. Texts are always a product of the author's viewpoints and opinions, and understanding a little about the author's background and credentials can help you understand the text.

- Pay attention to headings and subheadings in a text. They give you clues about what is being discussed. You may also find it helpful to write out your own outline, including chapter titles, headings, and subheadings, as you read so that you can map the structure of the text.

- The more you read, the better reader you will be. (The same is true of writing.) It is truly just that simple. The research in reading and writing theory also conclusively indicates that rote instruction in spelling, grammar, sentence structure, and vocabulary does not help students learn these concepts. The simple act of reading is what makes proper spelling, grammar, and sentence structure sink in naturally, and building vocabulary through reading is much more effective than activities like studying vocabulary lists and taking spelling tests. It does not even matter what you read. Magazines, newspapers, comic books, all types and genres of fiction . . . just pick something up and read if you are interested in being a better thinker, writer, and student. Of course, the more challenging the reading, the more potential there is for your intellectual development.

Exercise 3

Respond in writing to the following questions. Your instructor may ask you to hand in your responses.

A. Revisit the Zoellner and Tan essays. Write your personal and academic connections, knowledge questions, and global questions that arise after rereading the texts.

B. Which personal connections could you develop into your own essay? What might your purpose be?

C. What global questions could you develop into your own essay? What might your purpose be?

D. What information would you need to research in order to fill in your knowledge gaps?

Final Thoughts

There is much to balance in successful college writing: awareness of the objectives you must reach; understanding the criteria on which you will be graded; experimenting with different composing processes; the interplay of purpose, audience, and thesis in your sources and your own writing; and close, careful reading of source texts. In this course, we will try to explore all these dimensions of successful writing—as well as other elements.

You can probably see that this is not easy, and it takes a lot of practice: practice writing for various purposes and audiences, practice with different composing strategies and rituals to find what works best in a given situation, and practice reading what other successful writers have written. In English 101, you will practice all of these on your way to developing the skills and strategies of a confident and successful writer.

Works Cited for Chapter 1

Hacker, Diana. *A Pocket Style Manual.* 4th ed. Boston: Bedford/St. Martin's, 2004.

Reid, Stephen. *The Prentice Hall Guide for College Writers.* 6th ed. Upper Saddle River NJ: Prentice Hall, 2003.

Widmayer, Sharon Alayne. "'Schema Theory': An Introduction." *George Mason University Graduate School of Education Website.* 8 Jan 2006. <http://chd.gse.gmu.edu/immersion/knowledgebase/strategies/cognitivism/SchemaTheory.htm>.

Chapter 2: Reading & Responding to Texts

The Skills of Close Reading and Response

In a 2002 study, we asked CMU faculty what skills and knowledge students most needed to successfully write in college and beyond; we also asked faculty to rate the abilities of their current students on these skills and knowledge. According to most faculty surveyed, critical thinking is the most important skill students need, and it involves reading actively, understanding what is read, and then translating that understanding into coherent arguments. (Faculty also commented on the need for research skills, which are closely related to critical thinking, because research involves not only locating information, but also reading, understanding, and synthesizing it into one's own work.) Faculty also felt that even students in upper-level courses were relatively weak in these areas. Because the skills of summary and synthesis are so central to success in college-level work and in writing on the job after college, we begin the course with reading and response and build on that throughout the course.

Active, critical reading is naturally tied to writing, and the two are integrally related (discussion is a third element of this critical reading triad). That is, writing assists you in making sense of what you read, and discussion and active reading help you to formulate the content for your own essays.

Why Write a Reflective Response?

There are many possible ways of responding to our reading. For the first assignment, you will write a *reflective response* to an essay. You will rely not only on the text you read, but also on the personal connections that reading fosters. Personal experience forms the basis for many kinds of writing. When you are trying to persuade, you often tell what has happened to you as evidence for the point you are trying to make. When you do a lab experiment, you tell what you did and what happened as a result. When you arrive at a conclusion, you tell how you got there. Because reflections are based largely on personal experience, you are already an expert on the information, so this kind of essay makes a logical starting point for an introductory course in composition.

However, reflection is not as easy as simply telling a story or telling what you think. It involves synthesizing ideas and conveying a sense of their significance; in short, it involves *interpretation.* Reflective writing, like autobiography, comes out of experience and memory. It expands on autobiography, however, by exploring the larger *meaning* of events. As Stephen Reid explains,

> Direct observations are important to learning and writing, but so are your memories, experiences, and stories. You may write an autobiographical account of part of your life, or you may recall a brief event, a person or a place just as an example to illustrate a point. Whatever form your writing from memory takes, however, your initial purpose is to remember experiences so that you can understand yourself and your world. The point is not to write fiction, but to practice

19

drawing on your memories and to write vividly enough about them so that you and others can discover and learn. (104)

Thus, although reflection may rely on personal experience and use narration and description as strategies for development, it always has to go beyond the completely individual or personal. Once you have discovered what the memory has taught you, your task is to teach others through your writing. This is not easy, and it takes practice.

Another pair of writing teachers, Rise Axelrod and Charles Cooper, explain how reflective writing differs from strict autobiographical or observational writing:

> Autobiographers and observational writers often suggest larger meanings in what they show, but they seldom explore such meanings directly and in detail. In reflection, however, the focus shifts from showing to telling. Writers present something they did, saw, overhead, or read in order to tell us what they think it suggests about people and society. (117)

You are going to practice this crucial way of thinking and remembering by using another writer's ideas as a *trigger*. College coursework requires critical reading skills—you need to be able to summarize, analyze, and respond to a wide variety of texts, so we are starting with a writing activity that requires you to begin by reading critically. This assignment will help you to use reading—along with observation and memory—as a source for your writing.

Annotation

As we previously mentioned, annotation involves writing notes and questions as you read, using the margins of the text or a separate sheet of paper. You can start this process by previewing a text (read any supplementary introductory material provided, preview your own knowledge on the subject by writing a short journal entry, research the author's background, etc.).

Once you start reading, read through the text first for basic information and to get a feel for the style and subject matter (i.e. skim), making notes as you go. Then, read the piece a second time, underlining sections that seem particularly important or especially difficult. Note where you agree or disagree with the author, or mark places where you remember stories from your own experience that seem to confirm or refute the author's claims. You can circle words or phrases that need to be defined and put question marks next to passages that are confusing. In the margins, summarize paragraphs briefly, note responses or questions you have, identify interesting writing strategies the author has used, and point out patterns in the essay.

Another way to annotate is to do a *double-entry reading journal*, which is a way of taking notes that both records main ideas and features and comments on those passages and ideas. To begin, draw a line down the middle of a sheet of paper (you can do this by hand or on a computer); on the left side at the top, write "Summary Comments," and on the right side, write "Responses and Questions." As you come across key points or passages in the reading, write/type them on the left. After you have finished, go back and write/type any reactions or connections you have in the column across from them. This takes a little more time than annotation in the margins, but it is immensely useful in preparing to write about something you've read.

Summary

You have all probably learned how to summarize in past English classes, but it is a skill that needs lots of practice, and most new college students are not very good at summarizing longer and more complex readings. They seem mostly to know how to write plot summaries of short stories and novels but have difficulty summarizing nonfiction works, such as arguments or research reports. Before you can write about anything you read, you have to be able to understand its main point.

Written summaries are often used in our writing to introduce another person's ideas before we comment on those ideas or use them in our own arguments. Summaries (sometimes called abstracts or executive summaries) frequently appear at the beginning of published articles (especially research articles) so that readers can get a sense of what the article is about before they actually read it. At other times, summaries are the main focus of entire articles and books, such as annotated bibliographies. Most book reviews include a brief summary of the book being reviewed, sometimes at the very beginning of the review, sometimes not. And research databases, such as those accessible through the Park Library's web site, often include summaries of the various sources available in the database.

Developing a Summary

When you summarize, keep the following tips in mind:

- Early in the summary, give the author's name and the title of the text you are summarizing.

- Make your summary comprehensive, concise, coherent, independent, accurate, and objective (Spatt 93 - 116). Don't comment on or evaluate the author's ideas; just retell them.

- Make your summary an appropriate length for your audience and purpose. Summaries can be anywhere from a couple of sentences to a couple of pages, depending on the length of the source and the purpose of the summary. For our purposes, though, your summaries of short essays should be about 50 - 100 words (roughly one paragraph).

- It helps some writers to first outline the essay they plan to summarize—you can do this in the margins as part of your annotations.

- Tell readers what the main idea of the text is—there may be multiple key ideas, but keep in mind that you are trying to capture the main points, not every detail or example the author discusses. Get to the *central* point(s) of the piece. Focus on the forest, not the trees.

- Develop a *topic sentence,* and then develop subsequent sentences that elaborate on the topic sentence.

- You may directly quote a few key ideas, but only if the language is so compelling and already so concise that paraphrasing would not do it justice. Otherwise, paraphrase. (If you do quote, follow this rule of thumb: no more than 10% of the total number of words in your summary should be quoted material from the essay.)

- Be sure to refer to the author and his or her purpose so that the reader knows you are summarizing another person's ideas and not stating your own. (For instance,

"According to Walker…" or "As Walker argues…" If you are using Graff and Birkenstein's *They Say, I Say,* it provides lots of sample templates to help you learn how to refer to authors.)

- Use *active verbs* to describe what the author *does* in the essay, e.g., *shows, describes, states, explains, argues.* Avoid words and phrases such as *says* and *talks about.*

- Use *objective, neutral language.* Be aware of the connotations of the words you use—they will betray your biases, and in a summary, no bias should be apparent.

Sample Summary

The following is a summary one of us wrote for of an article by Timothy Ferris, "Interstellar Spaceflight: Can We Travel to Other Stars?" (Rpt. in Spatt). The summary is about 100 words. How many features of an effective summary can you identify?

> In his article, "Interstellar Space Flight: Can We Travel to Other Stars?," Timothy Ferris examines the future of space exploration. Specifically, he questions the feasibility of human interstellar space travel, pointing out the prohibitive cost of fuel and the extreme length of time it would take to travel to even the nearest stars. Ferris notes that, although there is no concrete evidence of alien civilizations, the most cost-effective method for discovering and communicating with them is through the use of small, unmanned space probes, which he believes could be used to establish an interstellar database to which all galactic civilizations would contribute and have access.

Exercise 4

Read the essay on Blackboard by Roger Sipher titled "So That Nobody Has To Go To School If They Don't Want To." Then do the following:

A. Print a copy of the essay, and annotate it in the margins.

B. Write a 50 – 100 word summary of the essay. Don't forget to refer to the author and what he *does* in the essay.

C. Write a paraphrase of the last paragraph of the essay. Again, don't forget to refer to the author and what he *does* in the passage.

Your instructor may ask you to hand in your responses.

Exercise 5

In Chapter 6, read the essay by Jenny Hung, titled "Surviving a Year of Sleepless Nights." It was written when Hung was a high school senior, and it appeared in the "My Turn" section of *Newsweek* in 1999. As you read it, *annotate* the essay directly in the margins. Then write a one-paragraph *summary* of the article (either typed or handwritten, according your instructor's directions); attach it to the annotations and be ready to discuss both. Your instructor may ask you to hand in your response.

Ways of Responding

In college, you will be asked to respond to texts in one of three usual ways:

1. by reflecting on the text,

2. by analyzing the way the text *works* in some way, or

3. by agreeing or disagreeing with the author's argument.

For Assignment 1, you will focus on the first mode of response: reflection. In Assignment 2, you will respond in the second way, by analyzing the rhetorical effectiveness of an essay. And in English 201, you'll learn to respond to multiple texts to make your own argument.

Although all these methods of responding require evidence, *reflection* asks you to make connections to *personal experiences and ideas* to a greater degree than the others do. For Assignment 1, you will try to draw on past experiences that connect with the essay you are reading. You will also rely on *textual evidence* to develop your reflections, directly quoting from the essay and paraphrasing key ideas on which you want to comment. (Note: Another strategy is to use evidence from other texts as well, which you may do in this assignment if you wish.) In reflecting on another author's essay, you are in a sense *interpreting* that essay for your readers, in light of what you know and think. That interpretation should explain ideas in a new way, to illuminate the essay's concepts by providing a new context in which to read them.

Exercise 6

Respond in writing to the following questions that ask you to practice constructing reflections based on your reading. Your instructor may ask you to hand in your responses.

A. Reread your annotated version of "Surviving a Year of Sleepless Nights." Spend 10 minutes *freewriting* on a passage you underlined in that essay as being particularly important, interesting, or questionable. Write quickly and without editing your thoughts.

B. Now, make a two-column chart (similar to the double-entry reading journal mentioned earlier) to help you move from key ideas or passages in Hung's essay to personal experiences that you can relate to them. In the left-hand column, list *triggers* or *occasions* from the Hung text—these could be stated as ideas or as quoted passages. In the right-hand column, list personal experiences that relate to these ideas. (Another option is to create a three-columned page: one column for the trigger from the Hung essay, the middle column for experiences that relate to the trigger, and the third column for comments/questions/interpretations that connect to a larger significance.)

Assignment 1

Select one essay from the group of readings provided by your instructor, and write a 4 – 6 page *reflective* essay triggered by some aspect of the essay you select. In your response, you will combine evidence from the essay, as well from your personal experience, to develop your reflections. Don't assume that your readers have read the essay to which you are responding.

Your instructor will either provide three or more essays on Blackboard or will ask you to write about one of the three essays on pages 139 – 161 in *They Say, I Say*.

Then, choose the essay you would like to respond to—pick one that you think is really well written and interesting. You will need to describe the *trigger* (i.e. the "occasion") vividly by summarizing or paraphrasing from the essay so that readers will understand what prompted your reflective response. (Note: If you *do* quote from the essay, do so very sparingly. No more than 10% of your essay should consist of quoted material. Use summary and paraphrase instead.)

In reflecting on the trigger, explore both your own values and society's dominant attitudes. You are writing not just for yourself but to share your thoughts with others and to stimulate their thinking, as well as your own.

Your instructor will provide additional formatting details.

Getting Started

1. Annotate, preview, and summarize your chosen essay. It is useful to share annotations and summaries with others, particularly those writing in response to the same essay.

2. Once you have tentatively narrowed the subject for your reflection, do some prewriting to develop your reflection on the subject. Use the following questions from *Reading Critically, Writing Well* (Axelrod and Cooper 155) if you need help:

   - **Generalize about it:** *Consider what you have learned from the essay that will be the occasion for your reflections/ideas.* What does it suggest to you? What does it suggest about people in general or about the society in which you live?

   - **Give examples of it:** *Illustrate your subject with specific examples.* Think of what would help your classmates understand the ideas you have about it (examples from your experience). Make a list of memories that could be illustrative.

   - **Compare and contrast it:** *Think of a subject that compares with yours.* Explore the similarities and differences.

- **Extend it:** *Take your subject to its logical limits.* Speculate about its implications. Where might it lead?

- **Analyze it:** *Take apart your subject.* What is it made of? How are the parts related to one another? Are they all of equal importance? Are there causes and effects you can isolate?

- **Apply it:** *Think about your subject in practical terms.* How can you use it or act on it? What difference would it make to you and to others?

Developing the Reflective Essay

Once you have determined the general trigger for your piece (Axelrod and Cooper refer to this as the "occasion" for a reflection), you need to work on developing your reflection. Your reflection or interpretation is the most important element of the essay. Developing these reflections is not easy, however. You cannot simply quote a passage from the trigger essay and then tell a story about yourself that relates to that passage. Readers have to see a *purpose* to your telling the story, and they have to have details and explanations to help them see the connections between the original trigger essay and your essay on it.

Axelrod and Cooper clarify how you create the connections for readers while you are developing your reflections:

> An occasion [or trigger] introduces a subject, and reflections explore the subject. Reflections include both ideas about self and society and development or exploration of those ideas. What does it mean to explore or develop ideas? It means simply to examine the ideas inventively in any way that illuminates them; for example, by giving examples, posing questions, or comparing and contrasting. In addition, the writer of a reflective essay might examine an idea by placing it in a surprising context—saying what it is not, associating it with other ideas, speculating about where it came from, trying to apply it, taking it seriously or taking it lightly. (124)

Start your drafting process by reading the essays and student responses referred to in Exercise 7 and carefully analyzing how the student writers approached the task. Then, try taking your annotations, summary, and other prewriting and using them to start writing a draft. Once you have finished a couple of paragraphs, stop and focus on developing the reflections in those sections before moving on (some writers prefer to write a complete first draft and then go back to develop it).

Exercise 7

Read the two pairs of essays referred to as "Reflection Set 1" and "Reflection Set 2" in Chapter 6. Each set begins with an essay by a professional writer and is followed by a reflective response. Then respond in writing to the following questions. Your instructor may ask you to hand in your responses.

A. What do you learn about your own experiences from reading Alice Walker's essay? What about Andrea Devenney's? Make a list of possible ways in which your experience connects to Walker's. (You might start by considering key *themes* that her story illustrates.)

B. Find passages in which Walker is writing *reflectively* about her experience. Discuss techniques Walker uses to develop her reflections. How could you borrow some of these techniques in your own piece?

C. How does Devenney attempt to blend her experience with textual evidence from Walker's essay? Where could she include *more* evidence to make her response even stronger? (Find passages in the Walker essay that Devenney could *quote* to add authority and depth to her reflections.)

D. Barbara Ehrenreich's essay is more of an *argument* than Walker's, which is a narrative with some commentary on that narrative. What methods lend themselves to responding to an argument like Ehrenreich's?

E. What approach to response did Jonathan Edwards take in responding to Ehrenreich's essay? Find places in his text where he comments directly on something triggered by Ehrenreich's essay. How does he respond?

F. Note the kinds of evidence Edwards uses: Where does he rely on experience? What about textual evidence?

G. Which response essay do you think is more effective, Edwards' or Devenney's? Why?

Peer Revision Workshop Questions for Assignment 1

Revision means "re-seeing," and that is exactly what writers try to do: to take another look at the large issues in their drafts and make sure the content and organization are set before finally editing, proofreading, and printing a final version. Obviously, it is crucial that writers become adept at re-seeing their own drafts, but to do that, they often benefit from getting feedback from others. Your instructor will respond to your work-in-progress and so will your peers. By reading your classmate's work, you also become a stronger, more critical reader of your own writing.

Read your classmate's draft once without making any comments. Then, read it through a second time and respond in writing to the following questions. Attach your written responses to the author's draft.

- How effectively has the writer used *summary* in the reflection? Has he or she identified the author and referred to the author so that you know which parts are summarized and/or paraphrased? Has the writer stayed fairly objective and focused only on the main ideas? If not, suggest places where the writer needs to revise.

- Underline places where the writer has *reflected* on some trigger from the original essay. How well does the writer develop these reflections? Where could the piece use more development? Suggest ways the writer could develop his or her reflection.

- Has the writer used *evidence from the original essay* to support his or her reflection? If not, indicate places where direct quotes or paraphrases would be useful in developing the argument.

- Point to places in the essay that particularly draw you in, inspire you to think, or challenge your beliefs or values. How could the essay more fully engage the interest of readers?

Exercise 8

Reflection is a skill you will use throughout college and beyond. In this class, you will often be asked to reflect on your own progress as a writer. Let's practice here by reflecting a bit on this first assignment. Your instructor may ask you to hand in your responses.

A. What questions do you still have about annotation, summary, paraphrase, and quoting?

B. What active reading strategies do you think are the most important for you as a writer/student? What reading strategies did you learn during this assignment?

C. How comfortable did you feel writing about your own experience in response to the reading? Do you think your gender, social class, or ethnic group has influenced the ideas you came up with? In what ways?

Works Cited for Chapter 2

Axelrod, Rise B., and Charles R. Cooper. *Reading Critically, Writing Well: A Reader and Guide.* 5th ed. Boston: Bedford/St. Martin's, 1999.

Reid, Stephen. *The Prentice Hall Guide for College Writers.* 6th ed. Upper Saddle River NJ: Prentice Hall, 2003.

Spatt, Brenda. *Writing From Sources.* 6th ed. Boston: Bedford-St. Martin's, 2003.

Chapter 3: Rhetorical Analysis

What Is Rhetoric?

The word *rhetoric* has several meanings, but the one that is pertinent to our endeavors is this one, from the *Oxford American Desk Dictionary and Thesaurus:* "art of effective or persuasive speaking or writing; language designed to persuade or impress" (719). A rhetorical analysis essay, therefore, is one in which you will analyze and evaluate the components of an author's persuasive writing.

Most people understand that it is very difficult to completely change an audience's mind on a subject. Therefore, when someone constructs an argument, whether orally or in writing, he or she does so with the purpose of *persuading the audience that a point of view is worth taking seriously*. To accomplish that goal, an author must choose his or her rhetoric carefully on all levels, from individual words to ideas to the organization of those ideas.

Why Analyze and Evaluate Rhetoric?

Argumentation and persuasion permeate our lives: the news media, television, film, novels, magazines, the Internet, the business world, advertising, our friends, our families, our teachers. In one form or another, all of these present arguments to persuade us to accept some viewpoint and/or to act in some way. The ways in which they construct their arguments—the *rhetoric* they choose—depends on what they are attempting to accomplish.

By analyzing rhetoric, then, we can better understand not only how arguments are meant to persuade us (and, if necessary, how we can respond to or resist those arguments), but also how we might make use of the same rhetorical techniques in our own writing. You will learn some basic *rhetorical features* or *techniques* that writers use to construct their arguments. These concepts will give you a basis for building your own persuasive essays and for evaluating the strengths and weaknesses of other people's arguments. In Assignment 2, you will analyze and critique an author's rhetorical skills.

What Do We Mean by Evaluation?

Evaluation involves making reasoned judgments about something, in this case about the quality of an author's rhetoric. The key word here is "reasoned," which is *not* the same as unsupported opinion. We make judgments every day—about movies, about clothes, about our classes—but usually these evaluations don't go beyond "I like" or "I don't like." However, in academic and much nonacademic writing, readers will expect you to back up your judgments with solid reasons and with good evidence to support those reasons. The reasons are based on *criteria* for evaluating the text under scrutiny; those criteria must be generally accepted as appropriate for judging a text.

For this assignment, you will evaluate the rhetorical quality of an editorial. The criteria for judging that quality will revolve around the *rhetoric* the author uses. We will look at the features that fall under the category "rhetoric" and, therefore, what would be considered appropriate criteria for judging a written argument.

Exercise 9

Read the article in Chapter 6 titled "Where's the Beef," by Alan Herscovici, which appeared in the *Toronto Sun* newspaper in 1998. Your instructor will place another, more recent, article about vegetarianism on Blackboard. After you have read both articles, respond in writing to the following questions. Your instructor may ask you to hand in your responses.

A. Which author presents a stronger argument? Why?

B. Do your personal feelings about eating meat interfere with judging the quality of the arguments?

C. How would you compare the *tone* of the two articles?

D. Which author has a more difficult argument to make? If you consider that the challenge is to convince the reader to take the argument seriously, does Herscovici or the other author have a more difficult task? Why?

Exercise 10

Read the essay in Chapter 6 titled "My 60-Second Protest from the Hallway," by Emily Lesk. Because all analyses should start with active reading, use the skills you practiced during Assignment 1 to read the essay carefully.

After reading Lesk's piece, *annotate* it in the margins, and write a one- to two-sentence summary of it. Then respond in writing to the following questions. Your instructor may ask you to hand in your responses.

A. **Claim:** What is the author's thesis or central claim? Is it stated explicitly? If so, where?

B. **Organization:** How would you divide this essay with respect to beginning, middle, and end? What does the writer do in the beginning to get your interest and forecast the subject? How does the writer structure the middle of the essay? What does the writer do to signal that the argument has moved to a conclusion? Describe features that characterize each of these sections.

C. **Evidence & Development:** Are the paragraphs full of details and explanations of the significance of those details? Are you convinced? Is the amount and type of support sufficient? Is there too much or too little of a certain kind of support? Explain.

D. **Diction and Tone:** How would you characterize the author's tone of voice in this essay? Is the speaker intelligent? Folksy? Hard-driving? Laid-back? Angry? Funny? Describe the tone and cite examples to illustrate. Beyond the content of the article, *how* does the writer create that tone? Word choice? Humor? Witty wordplay? Complicated or very simple sentences? List all the strategies you think the author uses.

Criteria for Evaluation

Whenever you read an opinion piece in a magazine or hear rhetoric on television, you get a sense of whether you believe what the author is arguing. That sense, though, is usually more on an unconscious level. However, to write a successful rhetorical analysis, you have to make very conscious judgments and be able to support them by analyzing specific aspects of the author's rhetoric. The first thing you need, then, is some *criteria* with which to begin your analysis.

The Classical Rhetorical Appeals

A group of teachers in ancient Greece, known as the Sophists, were the first to actually teach and write about rhetoric, i.e. about how to persuade people to act or believe in certain ways. Rhetoric in ancient Greece focused on oral speech, not only because the abilities to read and write were limited to only the most educated persons, but also because most public decisions were made based on oral speeches, e.g. in court, in the citizens' assembly. Nowadays, of course, we rely much more heavily on writing than did the ancient Greeks.

Classical rhetoric uses the terms *ethos, logos,* and *pathos* (or *ethical, logical,* and *emotional* appeals) to describe three major elements of persuasion.

Ethos: Credibility

Most of the ancient Greeks simply taught rhetoric as an informal art or technique for speakers who might need to persuade citizens of the state to do something, but Aristotle "studied speakers and audiences, observed what proved to be effective, and systematized it. [...] For Aristotle, *ethos* was about building the credibility of the speaker before an audience, not about the speaker's inherent worth" (Smith 4 - 5).

To present an effective argument, an author has to be respected by the reader as a credible source. It would be very easy to determine whether an author is credible if every editorial started out with the author's résumé; then, the readers could see for themselves whether the author's background and education makes him or her qualified to make an argument about the given topic. We all know, however, that it's not that easy. Instead, we have to learn to look for the subtle clues an author leaves in the editorial itself that help build credibility (or not).

Two overarching factors of credibility are the author's *audience awareness* and *sensitivity to the issue* argued. If an author does not correctly evaluate the intended audience, he or she runs the risk of offending the reader; if an author does not understand the issue thoroughly, he or she will likely not be sensitive to the types of appeals and strategies that will work best in arguing the issue.

In *The Craft of Research,* Wayne Booth, Greg Colomb, and Joseph Williams describe *ethos*:

> Readers judge your argument not just by the fact you offer, but by how well you anticipate their questions and concerns. In so doing, they also judge the quality of your mind, even your implied character, traditionally called your *ethos*. Do you seem to be the sort of person who considers issues from all sides, who supports claims with evidence that readers accept, and who

thoughtfully considers other points of view? Or do you seem to be someone who sees only what matters to [himself/herself] and dismisses or even ignores the views of others?

When you acknowledge other views and explain your principles of reasoning [...], you give readers good reason to work *with* you in developing and testing new ideas. In the long run, the ethos you project in individual arguments hardens into your reputation, something every [writer] must care about, because your reputation is the tacit element in every argument you write. It answers the unspoken question [posed by readers], *Can I trust you?* That answer must be *Yes.* (117 - 118)

Authors can use a number of strategies to present a credible self-image or *ethos*. Sometimes they appeal to their own expertise, their moral or ethical character, their patriotism, and so on, and sometimes they appeal to their readers' sense of what is true, good, ethical, moral, and so forth. Authors also use two other appeals to enhance their credibility: *logos* (logic) and *pathos* (emotion).

Logos: Logic and Reason

Logos refers to logic or reason. An author is using *logos* when he or she includes facts, statistics, logical or scientific reasoning, and, often, just plain old common sense. Sometimes an author builds a case incrementally by stating premises and asking the reader to generalize: if the premises are true, then the conclusion must be true also.

Reasoning can be a good rhetorical strategy, but it can also be misleading. Just because the premises are true, that doesn't necessarily mean an author's conclusion is valid. For example, if an author were to claim that our society's morals have declined and that television viewing has increased, and then concluded that television viewing has caused weakened morals, that would be an example of faulty reasoning (in this case, *false cause*). One of the primary rules of sound reasoning is that *correlation* (i.e. two things happening at the same time) does *not* necessarily equal causation (i.e. one thing causing the other).

Whenever you come across examples of reasoning in an editorial (or any other text that informs or persuades), you have to carefully consider whether the author's conclusion follows logically from the premises given. You must also consider whether the author's premises (i.e. assumptions) are true. Here's an example of reasoning in Herscovici's article:

> Every plant and animal species naturally produces far more offspring than their environment can support to maturity. This 'surplus' provides for food for other species. Aboriginal people called this 'the cycle of life.' We now usually call it 'the food chain.' We are part of this cycle, like every other living organism on the planet.

This is a *logos* appeal designed to make eating meat seem natural, and therefore reasonable, for humans; if you follow Herscovici's reasoning—i.e. that an overabundance of offspring creates a surplus food supply for other species and that we are part of this food chain—then it seems like our responsibility to eat meat, or at least it seems like a fringe benefit of the natural order of the world.

This example leads to a perfectly logical conclusion drawn from the premises given, but that is exactly what the author wants the reader to believe. You must be very careful in evaluating logical reasoning. Ask yourself if there are other factors that might contribute to or detract from the author's conclusion. Even if the conclusion is valid, did the author outline enough premises to make the conclusion clear and reasonable? Are the author's premises valid?

Pathos: Emotion

Pathos is intended to elicit a specific emotional response from readers. Emotional appeals are a very broad category, and you should always consider to *which* specific emotion(s) the author is appealing. Some common emotions to which authors appeal are sympathy, empathy, shock, sadness, humor, fear, and guilt.

Authors must be careful not to exaggerate appeals to emotions; in fact, a common form of fallacious reasoning is known as the "inappropriate appeal to emotion." Many politicians and advertisers use inappropriate appeals to people's fears.

The Five As: Allusion, Analogy, Anecdote, Assertion, and Authority

Allusion

The *Oxford American Desk Dictionary* defines an *allusion* as a "reference, [especially] a covert, passing, or indirect one." An allusion is an indirect reference to a commonly known event, person, story, or piece of pop culture or history. Allusions can function as *ethos, logos,* and/or *pathos* appeals; it depends on the nature of the allusion and the author's purpose for using it. Here are some examples:

1. Herscovici: "Where's the Beef?" (This is an allusion to Wendy's commercials in the 1980s and 1990s.)

2. Quindlen: "Put 'Em in a Tree Museum." (This is an allusion to the song "Big Yellow Taxi" by Joni Mitchell.)

3. Quindlen: "The Culture of Each Life." (This is an allusion to the phrase "culture of life" that is circulated so often in today's political debates about abortion and stem cell research.)

4. "Political leaders expect others to 'respect their authority' even if they have not earned respect." (This is an allusion to Cartman on *South Park*.)

5. "You look sad today. Do you have a case of the Mondays?" (This is an allusion to the film *Office Space*.)

6. "Mr. Jones is a real Napoleon, isn't he?" (This could be either an allusion to the 19th century French leader or to the more recent film character, *Napoleon Dynamite*. Readers would have to rely on the context of the allusion to determine which is the appropriate reference.)

Allusions are a powerful way for an author to subtly create an association between his or her point and something familiar to the intended readers; in a way, allusions are also a type of metaphor (which is discussed a bit later). But allusions have to be carefully chosen with the audience in mind, because what is "commonly" known varies greatly by audience. For example, young people might not be familiar with allusions 1 and 2 above, and people uninterested in politics and social debate may not understand 3. The humor in *South Park* and *Office Space* is certainly not recognizable to many people. And since the release of the movie *Napoleon Dynamite*, any vague allusion to Napoleon certainly has some very humorous potential for misinterpretation.

When you find allusions in an editorial, consider audience appropriateness as well as reader association. Does the allusion create an appropriate appeal (allusions can appeal to logic, ethics, or emotions)? Does the allusion relate to the argument's topic? Is the author simply name-dropping to create the appearance of being cultured, knowledgeable, or well-connected?

Analogy

An *analogy* is a comparison of two different things, events, relationships, or situations for the purpose of "encouraging readers to assume that what is true about one thing is also true" about the other (Axelrod and Cooper 400). Here are some examples:

1. "Sodomy laws are part of a dark tradition in this country . . . In this, their closest corollary is the now reviled Jim Crow laws" (Quindlen "Getting").

2. "Poverty is an acid that drips on pride until all pride is worn away. Poverty is a chisel that chips on honor until honor is worn away" (Parker).

3. "Many have the attitude today toward development [of land for commercial and residential use] that we once had toward smoking: sure it's bad, but it won't be a problem for me" (Quindlen, "Tree Museum").

Like allusion, analogy can be used to make any type of appeal. If you look at the examples above, you will notice that the first is a *pathos* appeal, designed to make the reader afraid of eating meat. The second can be considered an *ethos* appeal; by equating sodomy laws with Jim Crow laws, the author wants the reader to connect the immorality of "separate but equal" to the injustice of sodomy laws. The last is a *logos* appeal, meant to make a connection between the negative effects of smoking and overdevelopment.

Some special types of analogies are *metaphors* and *similes*, which you probably learned about in high school. As you may recall, a metaphor is a comparison, often using a specific word or phrase, whereas a simile is a metaphor that contains the words *like* or *as*.

If they are relevant to the issue, appropriate for the audience, and make valid comparisons, analogies are a very strong rhetorical strategy. In deciding whether an analogy aids the argument, there are several questions you can ask yourself: Are the two things being compared sufficiently similar to each other? Does the comparison make sense? Is the analogy truly relevant to the topic that is being argued, or does it simply make a memorable statement that is not really a valid comparison?

Anecdote

An *anecdote* is a story—not necessarily about the author or any other real person. Anecdotes are a common rhetorical strategy, but there are dangers in relying too heavily on anecdotal support.

To clarify, consider Barry Glassner, a sociologist who has extensively studied fear in America and the role that the news media, politicians, advertising, and other factors have played in perpetuating irrational fears among the public. One particular technique he cites as influential is the use of isolated incidents that are intended to represent trends. This means that often when one or a few particularly shocking or sad incidents occur, newsmakers and politicians talk about the incidents as if there is a trend among similar incidents. For example, even though there were some school shootings in the 1990s, there has actually been a huge decline in school violence in the past 20 years. However, because the media paid so much attention to those isolated incidents, running photos, footage, interviews, and devoting much airtime to recounting the tragedies, the public perceived an *increase* in school violence.

What Glassner speaks of is *misuse* of anecdotal evidence. Although anecdotes can be powerful rhetorical tools in making emotional appeals, it is probably not the strongest argument if all an author can come up with to support a claim is stories about individual people. Such stories are not representative of the entire population. Misuse of anecdotal evidence is frequently the source of stereotypes and prejudices.

The following are examples of anecdotal support:

1. "Look at my hands, so cracked and red. Once I saved for two months to buy a jar of Vaseline for my hands and the baby's diaper rash. When I had saved enough, I went to buy it and the price had gone up two cents. The baby and I suffered on" (Parker).

2. "I will never forget a teacher who played that card to get the attention of one of my children. Our youngest, a world-class charmer, did little to develop his intellectual talents but always got by. Until Mrs. Stifter" (Sherry).

3. "Imagine driving down the road, windows rolled down and the wind blowing through your hair. You feel carefree and liberated behind the wheel, somehow in charge of your destiny because you can steer that car anywhere. Suddenly in the rearview mirror, you see a car speed up behind you, weaving in and out of its lane. It goes to pass, but swerves too far into the gravel on the shoulder and spins out of control. You slam on the brakes and jerk the wheel to the right in an effort to avoid the other car, but it's too late. The last thing you see is impact before the world goes black."

Notice the difference between the first two examples and the last one: 1 and 2 are all true stories, derived from lived experience; however, 3 is a different kind of anecdote: it is *hypothetical*. It is clearly not something the author or another person has actually experienced. Instead, it is a story spun from an imagined experience to illustrate a point. Hypothetical anecdotes can be very persuasive, especially if they persuade readers to consider the issue from a perspective they had not considered previously.

Assertion

Assertion can be considered the foremost rhetorical strategy, because it is the only strategy that is present in every argument. The *Oxford American Desk Dictionary* defines an assertion as a "declaration; a forthright statement." That simply means that an assertion is a statement the author makes with the expectation that the reader will *believe* it is true. Sometimes assertions are factual, but that's not always the case. Simply *saying* that something is true doesn't make it so. Often, an author will need to provide evidence to support his or her assertions. Consider these examples:

1. "[Vegetarians] have trouble explaining, however, why human health and longevity have improved steadily as animal products became more readily available throughout this century" (Herscovici).

2. "Americans are afraid of the wrong things" (Glassner).

3. Academic performance is negatively affected by poor sleep habits.

4. The death penalty is morally hypocritical.

Some of these assertions, such as 2 and 4, are obviously opinions. Most readers would want to see more evidence before they would accept them as legitimate. The others, however, sound fairly convincing. The reader might accept those assertions as fact, but the sentences themselves are only assertions—they do not offer any *evidence* of their truth. Too many unsupported assertions will undermine an author's credibility. Too many unsupported assertions is propaganda, not argument.

It might help to think of assertions as the main supporting points of an author's argument, (i.e. the reasons the author provides in hopes of convincing readers to accept his or her claim). Editorials are not organized in the same way as the traditional five-paragraph theme; if they were, though, the thesis would be the primary assertion and the topic sentences of each paragraph would make secondary assertions to support that thesis.

In conducting your rhetorical analysis, identify the author's assertions and determine which of the other rhetorical strategies the author uses to support the assertions. An editorial that relies too heavily on unsupported assertions can definitely be a problem. You will also need to judge whether the strategies used to support assertions are themselves effective.

Often, an author will make an assertion and follow it up with one or more *examples* that support the point the author is making. Here are some examples, including the assertion in italics and the supporting examples in bold. (Did you notice that we just made an assertion and are now following it up with examples?)

1. "[...] *today's meats are lean*. **Based on equal-size servings, tofu has more fat than a sirloin steak and only half the protein**" (Herscovici).

2. "*Methane [...] is produced by all sorts of decomposition of organic matter, including normal digestion (even by vegetarians).* **Main sources of greenhouse gases include wetlands, forest fires, landfills, rice paddies, the extraction of gas, oil and coal— and even termites**" (Herscovici).

3. "*Poverty is living in a smell that never leaves.* **This is a smell of urine, sour milk, and spoiling food sometimes joined with the strong smell of long-cooked onions**" (Parker).

When you are examining the effectiveness of argument by example, ask yourself if the examples the author has provided are valid. Does each one make sense? Is the list of examples complete enough to present a strong case? Are the examples themselves assertions that need to be supported by authority? (See the following discussion.)

Authority

No one is an expert in everything, and often people who write editorials are not leading authorities on the topics they write about. Authors who truly want to present a persuasive argument should be aware enough of their own shortcomings to support their points by citing more credible authorities. Using *authority* as a rhetorical strategy means using expert testimony, statistics, and/or facts from authoritative sources to support an assertion. Keep in mind that although authority *can* be a very strong technique, not all authority is equal.

For example, in 1 above, readers might ask, "*Who says* that tofu has more fat than a sirloin steak and only half the protein?" If the author is a nutritionist or medical doctor, then readers will be inclined to trust the author's expertise on this matter; however, if the author is not an expert in nutrition, readers will expect to see some kind of authoritative source cited, for example, "According to the American Dietetics Association, tofu has more fat than a sirloin steak and only half the protein." Unless your mother is a nutritionist or physician, it would not be equally authoritative to write, "My mom says tofu has more fat than a sirloin steak and only half the protein." (Sorry, Mom!)

To evaluate the credibility of an authority, you need to consider how much detail the author provides. Are some identifying details given that prove the source is indeed authoritative? Do any statistics cited come from a reputable person or organization, and how do you know? Are significant details of a study provided to prove its validity? Are facts credited to a particular researcher or research organization? If they are not credited, then any "facts" the author presents are really just assertions. If the author fails to provide enough authoritative details, then his or her credibility will suffer and could seriously mar the effectiveness of the overall argument. If the authority is indeed trustworthy, then the author should say so.

Here are some examples of authority used to support assertions:

1. "In a recent report by the Centre for Energy and the Environment at the University of Exeter in England [...], meat scores far better than vegetables in this environmental-impact scale" (Herscovici).

2. The Department of Health and Human Services sets the poverty level for a family of four at around $18,000 per year.

3. Six out of ten high school seniors have been sexually active.

The first two examples are fairly strong uses of authority. They each credit the source of information, and the sources are credible. A university source is very credible when it comes to vegetarian issues. Government agencies are usually solid sources of information about poverty, as they are based on official Census information. The last example, however, falls short. Just because there are numbers involved does *not* mean the source is reliable. In fact, in the last example, no source is cited for the information; therefore, it lacks credibility, and by association, any author who includes such an unsupported assertion in his or her argument also lacks credibility. Readers have no way of knowing whether the author has simply made-up the statistics.

Usually, authority is used to make a *logos* appeal. Facts, statistics, and expert testimony by their nature are logical and reasonable. For example, an author trying to persuade readers that we should stop using animals in medical and cosmetic research might cite authorities on computer models to show that we really don't need to use animals anymore, because computer models are just as effective; or an author might cite physiologists who claim that there aren't enough similarities between humans and animals to justify continued use of animals in research. In both cases, the use of authority would function largely as *logos* appeals to show readers that it's no longer reasonable to use animals in such research. By citing credible sources, the author also further enhances his or her own credibility.

However, you need to consider each example of authority on a case-by-case basis to decide what type of appeal the author is making. For example, again, in an argument against the use of animals in medical and cosmetic research, an author might include expert opinion from religious leaders, professors/scholars of ethics, and so on, all of whom would be cited less as *logos* appeals than as *ethos* or *pathos* appeals. In other words, an author would cite such authorities to help persuade readers that the use of animals for medical and cosmetic research is unethical and/or immoral.

If the author also cited sources that describe inhumane treatment of animals in the past and present, then those sources would function as *pathos* appeals, i.e. the author would be trying to elicit an emotional response from readers about such treatment (e.g. disgust, empathy for the animals, anger at the researchers, and so forth).

It is very important to remember that although we are used to looking for the hard evidence of authority as a sign of a strong argument, authority is definitely not the *only* effective strategy an author can use to back up his or her assertions.

Other Rhetorical Strategies

In addition to the Five As, you also need to consider an author's use of diction and tone, as well as how the author has organized his or her ideas.

Diction & Tone

Diction refers to an author's word choice, especially as it relates to the level of formality (i.e. diction) of the author's writing style. Through word choice and diction, an author creates a *tone.* Tone in writing is the same as tone of voice: sarcasm, seriousness, melodrama, humor, shock, anger, objectivity, and many other emotions or voices can all be conveyed with careful word choice. (Note: You have probably realized, then, that tone can also function as *ethos, logos,* or *pathos* appeals!)

Consider the following examples:

1. "Whoops! Sorry! Not supposed to call alcohol a drug!" (Quindlen, "Drug").

2. "Based on equal-size servings, tofu has more fat than a sirloin steak and only half the protein. (Tofu also makes a mess of the grill.)" (Herscovici).

3. "Three times a day, you make a decision that not only affects your quality of life, but the rest of the living world. We hold in our knives and forks the power to change this world" (Pace).

Quindlen's tone is very sarcastic; she definitely is *not* sorry for calling alcohol a drug. Herscovici is making an attempt at humor with his parenthetical comment, and Pace conveys a very serious, moral tone. Consider how a change in diction can cause the tone to change, but still keep the main ideas:

1. Many people and organizations are offended when anyone calls alcohol a drug.

2. Tofu has more fat and half the protein of a sirloin steak, and tofu is not nearly as easy to serve at family barbeques.

3. The next time you sit down to a meal, raise your knives and forks to a vegetarian choice—you won't be sorry!

An author's diction and tone are very important to building (or losing) credibility. The author has to choose a tone that is appropriate to the issue itself and suitable for the audience. Tone changes as an author moves through an argument, and making a poor choice might offend the reader or make the author appear as though he or she doesn't understand the issue well enough to set the right tone. For example, if the issue is as serious as terminal illness or abortion and the author uses a sarcastic, humorous tone, the reader would likely think the author is insensitive. (Of course, comedians deliberately use such "insensitive" approaches, but their purpose is not necessarily to persuade but to entertain. Still, comedians who misjudge their audience will bomb!) Similarly, being overly serious about a lighthearted topic will likely make readers think the author is a bore.

When you undertake your rhetorical analysis, you must learn to identify the word choices the author makes to create his or her tone and recognize any tone changes that are present in the piece. You then have to judge whether the tone is appropriate for the author's argument and intended audience (which may not necessarily include *you*).

Organization

The way an author organizes ideas can greatly affect his or her credibility. An author's choices in organizing ideas and determining where to place various rhetorical strategies can either help or harm his or her credibility. For example, consider the potential pitfalls of *pathos* appeals. Depending on the audience and argument, coming out too early with humor or fear might make the reader uncomfortable or it might be just the right appeal to put the reader in the proper frame of mind. Making appeals to values, such as patriotism, ethics, or morality can be tricky, too, because an author must assume that readers share those values and define them in the same way as the author does. If an author accurately reads the audience, placing these appeals early in an essay can be an excellent technique to create a bond with the reader; however, if the author has misjudged, then he or she will bomb, just as surely as comedians who misjudge their audiences. In some situations, an author might need to build credibility in other ways before making such appeals.

When you start your rhetorical analysis assignment (which is described after Exercise 13), try making a general outline of the editorial first; ask yourself if the author builds the argument in a progression that makes sense and if the order in which appeals are presented is a strength or a weakness in terms of helping establish the author's credibility.

Exercise 11

Evaluate the rhetoric of "Where's the Beef?" and the other article about vegetarianism your instructor placed on Blackboard. Make a copy of the essays. Using a pen and different colored highlighters for each of the rhetorical strategies, highlight the two articles. For example, underline the author's assertions, and use pink for authority, orange for analogy, yellow for allusion, green for anecdotes, blue for reasoning, and purple for examples. Be prepared to talk about your determinations with the class.

Then, respond in writing to the following questions. Your instructor may ask you to hand in your responses.

A. What are the main appeals made by Herscovici? By the other author? Which strategies are used to make those appeals? How successful are those appeals?

B. Which author is more credible? Why?

How Rhetorical Appeals and Strategies Overlap

Often, the lines blur between different appeals and strategies. In order to make a decision about which type of appeal or strategy an author is using, you usually have to look at word choice. For example, a simple change from the word *killed* to the word *euthanized* takes away much of the emotional impact (and in many situations, this change is exactly what's needed; in other cases, perhaps not).

For example, in the argument, "Adopt a puppy from an animal shelter to save the puppies from being euthanized," you might decide the author is trying to appeal more to the reader's morals (i.e. it's the right thing to do) than to the reader's sympathy (i.e. the poor puppies!); conversely, the opposite might be the case if the author had written, "Adopt a puppy from an animal shelter to save the puppies from being killed" or "murdered." Obviously, word choice can betray an author's biases, which may either enhance or detract from his or her credibility. It depends on the topic, the audience, and the purpose of the writing.

Authors can use a number of strategies to build their credibility *(ethos)* and demonstrate their awareness of the issues and of the needs and expectations of their readers (see Figure 4). In this section, you have learned about several common rhetorical strategies that authors use in making appeals and establishing their credibility. Some of these strategies are more common than others, and not every strategy is used in every piece of writing. The key to a successful rhetorical analysis is being able to recognize the strategies an author does use, determine what appeals are being crafted by the author's use of the strategies, and draw conclusions about whether the author's choices enhance his or her credibility and the strength of the argument.

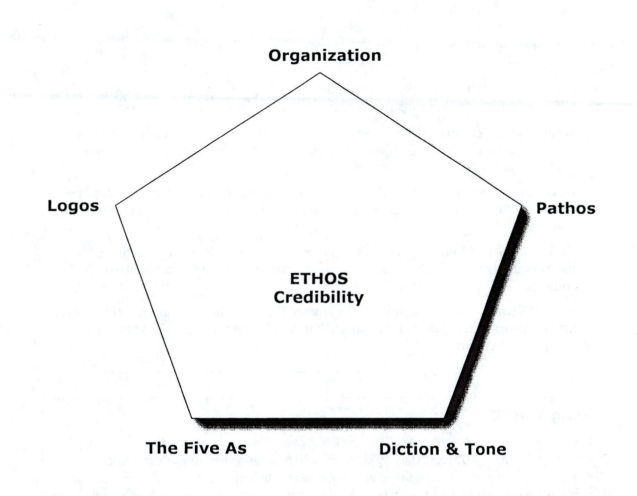

Organization

Logos

Pathos

ETHOS
Credibility

The Five As

Diction & Tone

Figure 4: The Elements of Ethos

Exercise 12

Read the two essays in "Rhetorical Analysis Set 1" in Chapter 6 and respond in writing to the following questions. Your instructor may ask you to hand in your responses.

A. What is Mary Rosalez's overall claim about the rhetorical effectiveness of Rick Reilly's editorial? How well do you think she makes her case? (Cite specific evidence that she uses.)

B. Imagine that you have to argue the *opposite* of Rosalez's claim regarding Reilly's editorial. What evidence would you use from his text? What are the most compelling features?

C. Evaluate the structure of Rosalez's argument: How has she organized her essay? Is it effective?

Read the two essays in "Rhetorical Analysis Set 2" in Chapter 6 and respond in writing to the following questions. Your instructor may ask you to hand in your responses.

A. What is Angie Fenton Freidman's overall claim about the rhetorical effectiveness of Richard Estrada's editorial? How well do you think she makes her case? (Cite specific evidence that she uses.)

B. Imagine that you have to argue the *opposite* of Freidman's claim regarding Estrada's editorial. What evidence would you use from his text? What are the most compelling features?

C. How well has Freidman supported her claims? Note particular spots where she has used textual evidence well. Also mark sections where you feel she could use more support.

D. Richard Estrada's piece appeared in the *Los Angeles Times* in 1995. Do you think, given his audience and the date of appearance, that the piece was effective? What about today, over a decade later?

Assignment 2

Choose an editorial from among those provided by your instructor on Blackboard, and write a 4 - 6 page (1,000 - 1,500 words) essay analyzing and evaluating the author's rhetoric. Although you may point out positives and negatives of the writer's rhetoric, you must make some overall judgment about the piece's effectiveness. In other words, you will be writing an argument.

Things to keep in mind as you prepare to write:

1. Select your editorial carefully. Choose one with details you can easily identify and write about. Choose a piece that you find interesting (if *you* do not find it interesting, chances are your reader will not find your analysis and evaluation of it interesting either).

2. To do well on this assignment, you will need to summarize the author's argument as well as discuss features of his or her rhetoric (i.e. you have to "prove" that the rhetorical features would either help or fail to convince the intended readers of the author's claim).

3. You will need to support your argument with specific examples from the text. You may get a very clear feeling about the tone and authority of a text, but you *must* be able to pinpoint where and how you got that feeling and why you think it is so successful or unsuccessful in persuading.

4. Remember that you, yourself, are making an argument—you should have a strong thesis that focuses on what you are trying to prove about the editorial and its rhetorical effectiveness.

Your essay should be double-spaced with 1" margins and a 12-point font. Your instructor will provide additional formatting instructions.

After selecting the essay you plan to analyze and evaluate, make sure you annotate and summarize it first. Then, respond in writing to these questions as a way to brainstorm ideas for your essay. Your instructor may ask you to hand in your responses.

A. **Claim:** What is the author's thesis or central claim? Is it stated explicitly? If so, where?

B. **Organization:** How would you divide this essay with respect to beginning, middle, and end? What does the writer do in the beginning to get your interest and forecast the subject? How does the writer structure the middle of the essay? What does the writer do to signal that the argument has moved to a conclusion? Describe features that characterize each of these sections.

C. **Evidence & Development:** How would you classify the rhetorical strategies that the author uses? For instance, think in terms of *ethos, logos,* and *pathos,* as well as the Five As (allusion, analogy, anecdote, assertion, and authority). Consider whether the amount and type of support is sufficient. Is there too much or too little of a certain kind of support? Explain.

D. **Diction and Tone:** How would you characterize the persona speaking in this essay? Does the author seem intelligent? Folksy? Hard-driving? Laid-back? Angry? Funny? Use your own words to describe the tone. Obviously, the nature of the claims that the speaker makes gives you some sense of his or her tone. But beyond the content of the article, *how* does the writer create that tone? Word choice? Humor? Witty wordplay? Complicated or very simple sentences? Use of statistics? Questions? Analogies? List all the *techniques* that the author uses, and cite specific examples of each.

E. **As a final step, do the following:** (1) draft a thesis that states your overall evaluation of the editorial, and (2) develop an outline of the body paragraphs that would then support your claim. Remember, you are constructing an argument in this assignment, so organization, evidence and development, and diction and tone apply to *you,* too. Therefore, take your time and consider your rhetorical choices carefully.

Drafting the Rhetorical Analysis

Now that you have practiced using the criteria for analyzing and evaluating an editorial, it is time to move on to the task of drafting your analysis into a complete and coherent essay. Four important concepts are involved in writing a successful rhetorical analysis essay: (1) summary of the author's argument, (2) analysis of rhetorical strategies, (3) judgment of the strategies' effectiveness, and (4) support for your judgment. Consider also how much of your essay should be allotted to each concept.

Introduction (about 10 – 15% of your paper)

The introduction must let readers know what you are writing about. As with all writing tasks, you have a purpose and an audience. For the audience of your paper, imagine that the newspaper or magazine or web site where the original editorial appeared has asked you to evaluate the writer's argument for an upcoming issue. Therefore, any reference to "the editorial I chose" or other references that assume that your class or the teacher is the audience would be inappropriate. Remember: Your purpose is to evaluate the author's rhetorical choices, i.e. *how* he or she constructs the argument and the effect that those choices create. Your purpose is *not to argue the issue itself.*

By imagining that you are writing an evaluation of the editorial to appear in the same publication, you will still need to provide your readers with some information:

- Provide background information about the editorial itself and its context, and summarize it as you learned to do in Chapter 2. Readers may or may not be familiar with the editorial you are evaluating, so you will have to provide sufficient information from the editorial. Even readers who have read it may have forgotten the key points and will appreciate the summary.

- State your own thesis about the overall effectiveness of the author's argument, and provide a brief overview of *your* argument in terms of your evaluation of the editorial's organization, the author's use of evidence and development (i.e. rhetorical strategies), and his or her diction and tone. (These are the analytical criteria you will focus on in the body of your essay.)

Your thesis must state your overall evaluation of the editorial's argument. Thus, you are making a *claim of value.* Your thesis could also include references to the criteria for making such an evaluation. The editorial probably won't be all good or all bad, so you will need to make a *qualified claim.*

An effective thesis should also answer the question, "So what?" In this case, the answer should be based on your analysis, i.e. the editorialist makes an effective or ineffective argument, and your analysis is important in pointing to the value of the piece and in adding to our knowledge of rhetoric and the subject of the editorial.

Here are some sample thesis statements. Compare these to the thesis statements in the Rosalez and Freidman essays—which do you think is "best" and why?

1. Although Smith makes a few assertions that he does not adequately support, his balanced use of anecdotal and statistical support; his organizational pattern, which increases the impact of the stories and statistics; and his witty, satirical tone combine to create a credible and effective argument.

2. Smith must never have considered his audience. His tone is aggressive when it should be calm and understanding; his support is almost entirely anecdotal when it should be logical and authoritative; what little logical support he has is flawed, full of generalizations. In short, the piece is a rhetorical disaster.

3. Although Smith's stories are entertaining, he lacks sufficient support, his organization seems random, and he adopts an inappropriate tone, thereby causing his argument and *ethos* to crumble.

Body: Analysis and Evaluation (about 70 – 80% of your paper)

It is logical to organize the body around the rhetorical features (note how the preceding thesis statements forecast the divisions of the body section of each essay around certain features in a certain order). Consider, for instance, the last sample thesis statement. If this were your paper, you would start with a section about Smith's entertaining stories. You would discuss how they are used, what the effect is, and why they are "entertaining." Then you'd make a transition to the rest of the body in which you would show how the piece is predominantly ineffective. Imagine that you will arrange these ineffective features from least to most important. Imagine that the deficiencies in support, organization, and tone build on one another to result in the most important deficiency of all: lack of credibility (weak *ethos*). This is, in fact, the order in which the analytical criteria are presented in the third sample thesis statement presented above.

Don't feel compelled to address *all* the rhetorical strategies, only those that are most relevant to the editorial you are analyzing and evaluating. Decide which criteria are appropriate for your analysis and evaluation. However, if you overlook an obvious strategy or seem not to recognize an author's failure to use an obvious strategy, then that will affect your grade on the assignment.

In each body paragraph (or section—some features may require more than one paragraph to adequately analyze), you should answer the following:

1. What is the rhetorical feature? In a sense, this becomes the topic sentence of the paragraph or section. Is it used effectively or ineffectively? Why do you think so?

2. What evidence from the text shows the use of this feature? (You must cite specific examples *from the text* as evidence; sometimes you will want to include more than one.)

3. What is the effect that is created by the author's choice to use this feature? Is it effective or ineffective? Why do you think so?

If a feature calls for a lot of examples or explanation, you may need two or more paragraphs to discuss the feature.

Present your analysis using well-developed paragraphs with clear topic sentences to signal to readers which of the analytical criteria you are addressing (and again, they should be addressed here in the same order you mention them in your thesis statement).

Conclusion: Overall Evaluation (about 10 - 15% of your paper)

Your conclusion should avoid simply summarizing the body of your essay. Again, an effective strategy is to hook back to the introduction in some way. Also, you can use another quote, a "kicker" quote that you see as summing up or showing the effectiveness or ineffectiveness of the editorial, and base your concluding remarks on it. You might also suggest examples of strategies that the author didn't use but probably should have, strategies that would have made the author's editorial more persuasive.

Peer Revision Workshop Questions for Assignment 2

Read your classmate's draft once without making any comments. Then, read it a second time and respond in writing to the following questions. Attach your written responses to the author's draft.

- To what extent has the author effectively introduced and summarized the editorial in the opening section? What do you think of the author's opening strategy? Is it interesting?

- Underline the author's *thesis*. Is it clear? Does it evaluate the rhetoric of the editorial and avoid arguing the issue? Does it forecast the features that will be addressed in the paper? Offer suggestions on how the author might make the introduction more effective and interesting.

- What is your evaluation of your classmate's use of evidence to support his or her claims about the effectiveness of the editorial? Give paragraph references to point out where the author needs to provide (1) more examples, (2) more *relevant* examples, or (3) clearer analysis of the examples' significance to the argument.

- How effective is the author's conclusion? If it's not very effective, suggest alternatives.

Final Thoughts

This introduction to rhetoric will equip you to construct arguments of your own. You are now familiar with a repertoire of rhetorical strategies to choose from as you write, particularly as you write academic papers that aim to inform and persuade. You should also feel more confident in asserting judgments, particularly about nonfiction texts, something you probably were not used to doing. Evaluating ideas based on logical criteria is a skill you will be asked to perform repeatedly in college and beyond.

Works Cited for Chapter 3

Axelrod, Rise B., and Charles R. Cooper. *Reading Critically, Writing Well: A Reader and Guide.* 5th ed. Boston: Bedford/St. Martin's, 1999.

Booth, Wayne C., Gregory G. Colomb, and Joseph M. Williams. *The Craft of Research.* 3rd ed. Chicago: U of Chicago P, 2008.

Crowley, Michael. " 'A' is for Average." *Readers Digest* Nov. 2004: 33-36.

Glassner, Barry. *The Culture of Fear: Why Americans Are Afraid of the Wrong Things.* New York: Basic Books, 1999.

Parker, Jo Goodwin. "What is Poverty?" *75 Readings Plus.* 6th ed. Eds. Santi Buscemi and Charlotte Smith. Boston: McGraw Hill, 2002.

Quindlen, Anna. "The Culture of Each Life." *Newsweek* 4 Apr. 2005: 62.

---. "The Drug that Pretends it Isn't." *Loud and Clear.* Apr. 2000. New York: Random House, 2004.
    83-86.

---. "Getting Rid of the Sex Police." *Newsweek* 13 Jan. 2003: 72.

---. "Put 'Em in a Tree Museum." *Newsweek* 13 Aug. 2004: 74.

Reid, Stephen. *The Prentice Hall Guide for College Writers.* 6th ed. Upper Saddle River NJ: Prentice
    Hall, 2003.

"Rhetoric." *The Oxford American Desk Dictionary and Thesaurus.* 2nd ed. London: Oxford UP, 2001.

Sherry, Mary. "In Praise of the F Word." *Models for Writers: Short Essays for Composition.* 7th ed. Eds.
    Alfred Rosa and Paul Eschholz. New York: Bedford/St. Martins, 2001. 445-447.

Smith, Craig. R. "*Ethos* Dwells Pervasively." *The* Ethos *of Rhetoric.* Ed. Michael J. Hyde. Columbia
    SC: U South Carolina P, 2004.

Chapter 4: Writing from Multiple Sources

What Is Research?

When most people hear the word *research,* they probably imagine scientists in a laboratory conducting experiments, or naturalists in the jungles of Africa or South America gathering specimens of as yet undiscovered flora and fauna. Those are certainly types of research, but far from the most common types. According to Booth, Colomb, and Williams, we all do research "whenever we gather information to answer a question that solves a problem" (10). The problem may be theoretical or practical. Perhaps you conducted research— albeit informally—in deciding what college to attend, or what car to buy with the $2,500 your grandmother left you, or where to spend your Spring Break, and so forth. If you're smart, you'll do some research as part of the process of selecting your major. These are all examples of *informal* research. In contrast, *formal* research is more systematic, but just as widespread.

> Teachers at all levels devote their lives to research. Governments spend billions on it, businesses even more. Research goes on in laboratories and libraries, in jungles and ocean depths, in caves and in outer space, in offices and, in the information age, even in our homes. Research is in fact the world's biggest industry. Those who cannot do it well or evaluate that of others will find themselves sidelined in a world increasingly dependent on sound ideas based on good information produced by trustworthy inquiry and then presented clearly and accurately. [...]
>
> Without trustworthy *published* research, we all would be locked in the opinion of the moment, prisoners of what we alone experience or dupes to whatever we're told. Of course, we want to believe that our opinions are sound, yet mistaken ideas, even dangerous ones, flourish because too many people accept too many opinions based on too little evidence. And as recent events have shown, those who act on unreliable evidence can lead us— indeed have led us—into disaster. (Booth, Colomb, and Williams 9 - 10)

In his book *The Transition to College Writing*, Keith Hjortshoj, a professor at Cornell University, offers practical advice to college students on how to adjust to the different expectations of the college setting. Although his book offers advice on many different issues related to college writing, his perspective on a "research paper" is particularly useful. With no disrespect to high school teachers, he explains the difference between their purpose in assigning a research paper (which is usually to give you *practice* in research methods) and college instructors' purposes in assigning research-based writing (which is primarily to develop your *intellectual* skills):

> Professors do not assign research papers just to make sure you can find and document references on a topic. They want to give you a taste of real scholarship in their fields of study, based on your own investigations. All of your professors are scholars who conduct research for the purpose of raising and answering *questions* in ways that will contribute to knowledge in their fields. These questions become significant within a larger *frame of reference* that includes the work of other scholars; for this reason scholarly

writing is always part of an *ongoing discussion.* Academic writers use quotation and citation not just to tell readers where they got their information, but more often to acknowledge the previous research, ideas, and arguments of other participants in the discussion. (155)

In essence, Hjortshoj sums up the challenge of learning to acclimate yourself to the academic culture, where research is used to situate your ideas in a broader framework of previous ideas and findings about a given topic, *not* to merely support your ideas with quotes from other sources. In their book *They Say, I Say,* Gerald Graff and Cathy Birkenstein echo this sentiment:

> The underlying structure of effective academic writing—and of responsible public discourse—resides not just in stating our own ideas, but in listening closely to others around us, summarizing their views in a way that they will recognize, and responding with our own ideas in kind. Broadly speaking, academic writing is argumentative writing, and we believe that to argue well you need to do more than assert your own ideas. You need to enter a conversation, using what others say (or might say) as a launching pad or sounding board for your own ideas. (3)

What is Synthesis?

For the previous two writing assignments, you have responded critically and analytically to *one* text. However, synthesis requires you to apply those critical and analytical skills to *a number of related texts* and bring those texts together in "conversation" with one another.

The word *synthesis* is defined by the *Oxford American Desk Dictionary* as a "combining of elements into a whole." In this way, synthesis is similar to what you probably learned in high school if you wrote a research paper, in that you will choose texts that relate to a single topic or issue and combine the ideas from those texts into a whole essay. However, to understand what a synthesis is, it is important to reconceptualize what "research" is and, in the process, come to understand what is expected of your writing in college.

Although synthesis is research-based, it is much more than what you probably think of when you hear "research." Synthesis requires that you *earn* your right to enter into an "ongoing discussion" about a particular topic by researching what others say about it— both those who agree and those who disagree with you—and showcasing their ideas as prominently as your own.

The following sections offer detailed information on how the process of researching and synthesizing ideas for an essay differs from the kinds of research-based writing you may have done in high school. (This doesn't mean your high school writing wasn't useful, only that the job of your high school teachers was to lay a foundation of basic research and writing skills, skills that you must build on now by enhancing and intensifying your *intellectual* skills—that is, learning to *think* in more sophisticated ways and reflect that sophistication in your writing.)

Researching a Topic for a Bibliographic Essay

A bibliographic essay is different from a "research paper" in the way you approach your research. Consider the example of Steve, a strong writer who took four years of English in high school. When Steve was assigned a research paper in his senior English class, he started by deciding what he wanted to write about. He chose the death penalty, because he felt very strongly that it should be abolished. He went to his school library and searched the databases using a keyword search of "death penalty," and he used Google for the same search. Using the sources he found, he wrote a simple, five-paragraph style essay that argued three reasons we should not have the death penalty: its bias against the poor, its lack of room for error, and its moral hypocrisy. He used sources to support those three reasons, and he received a good grade on the research paper because he fulfilled all of his high school teacher's requirements—thorough documentation of sources and an organized format to the essay.

A bibliographic essay requires considerably different research methods. When Steve got to English 101 at CMU, he was assigned to write a bibliographic essay, and he decided to revisit the topic of the death penalty. He submitted a minimally revised version of his high school essay as his rough draft and was surprised when his instructor, Dr. Anderson, told him he would have to completely rewrite the essay. She explained that Steve did not examine the issue from a wide enough perspective. Because Steve presented only one side to the issue and did not examine any of the broader historical or societal aspects of capital punishment, his rough draft was far too simplistic.

Dr. Anderson suggested that Steve broaden his search criteria, investigating issues of the legal system, race, history, morality, and politics to create a wide understanding of the complexity of the death penalty debate. She wanted Steve to look beyond the Internet and search for books and contemporary journal and magazine articles that relate to those facets of the issue. When Steve broadened his research, he gained a much better understanding of the *debate as a whole*, rather than just reinforcing the opinion he already had about the death penalty. In Steve's case, his opinion about the issue did not change, but he *earned* the right to have an opinion about it that other people would respect, because he had researched it, read about it, and thought critically about the many different perspectives on the death penalty.

You can learn from Steve's experience, because for your bibliographic essay, you need to start with a topic, issue, or concept and find sources that will help you exhibit a broad understanding of the debate over that topic. A bibliographic essay requires you to research a wide variety of sources (e.g. books, periodicals, web sites, films, television and radio shows) that relate directly or tangentially and find the similarities and the differences among those sources in terms of the points at issue in the debate. Instead of a direct argument about one side of your topic, a bibliographic essay presents a more far-reaching perspective, examining all sides and branching out into related issues that help shed light on the topic.

(Note: In all research, we must guard against the fallacy of the *false dilemma*, also known as the *either/or* fallacy. Most issues of consequence have more than two sides, so if you oversimplify an issue into only two sides, you are guilty of fallacious reasoning, which is a serious breach of critical thinking. In fact, some issues—such as whether the Holocaust happened or whether humans walked on the moon—have only one side, and anyone who does not accept that fact of history is either ignorant or irrational.)

Reading and Using Sources

Another significant way that a bibliographic essay is different from a "research paper" is in how sources are used in the essay. In a research paper, sources are used independently of one another to support the main points the author wants to make about the topic. Typically, the author's own ideas take center stage, and the sources are used to lend credibility, support, and detail to those main ideas. When Steve wrote his high school paper on the death penalty, he picked out quotes and paraphrases from the sources *that supported the views he already had on the issue.* He considered only the way the sources related to *his* thoughts, not the way the sources related to *each other.*

A bibliographic essay, on the other hand, uses the sources themselves as the focal point of the essay. Instead of the sources being used to supplement the author's ideas, the ideas in the sources *are* the main ideas of the essay, and the sources come together to "discuss" your topic. In English 101, when Steve broadened his research on the death penalty, he started to notice that many sources brought up the same points but that sometimes even sources on the same side of the debate disagreed about certain points. Instead of using the sources to support his opinions, *the points of agreement and disagreement became the focus of the body of his paper.* Instead of making his own assertions about the death penalty, Steve started using phrases like "Some people against the death penalty seem to be in agreement about...," "According to Smith...," and "Brown supports Smith's point using..." Although he still agreed and disagreed with certain authors, he inserted his opinions *into the larger debate* rather than making his opinions center stage. As a result, his paper became much stronger, and he, as the author, became much more credible.

To better conceptualize the way sources are used in a bibliographic essay, it helps to reconsider the way we think about sources. Margaret Kantz, a professor at Central Missouri State University, recognizes that "students expect factual texts to tell them 'the truth' because they have learned to see texts statically, as descriptions of truths, instead of as arguments" (192). In other words, because of years of being trained to read that way, when you pick up a text, you usually see it as a collection of facts instead of reading it as an author's point of view. When we see sources that way, it is easy to use the "facts" in those sources to back up our viewpoints. We simply figure out what we want to say and find a source to support it.

A successful bibliographic essay requires a new kind of reading skill. You need to apply the same scrutiny to your bibliographic essay sources that you applied to the editorial you used for your rhetorical analysis. You know that the editorial represents an author's viewpoint, so you treated that text as one voice, not "truth." It is easy to think of a text as an author's voice if it is blatantly an opinion piece, but we often don't think of other texts that way.

In reality, *all* texts represent an author's voice and viewpoints. Even sources that sound like they are reporting facts are really reporting the author's perception of the topic at hand. Consider how two people who witness the same event can give very different accounts of the event depending on their perspectives or how differently people can react to the same joke, movie, or song. For example, after watching Chris Farley's sketch on *Saturday Night Live* of motivational speaker Matt Foley, one person might find Farley's over the top, physical comedy hilarious, whereas someone else might be annoyed by Farley's yelling. Each person, therefore, would provide a very different interpretation of the *SNL* sketch. Just as our understanding of the world is informed by our pasts, our opinions, our moods, and our dreams, when an author sits down to write, the text he or she produces is influenced by the same factors and is furthermore influenced by the author's purpose in writing and his or her intended audience.

Consider the changes that have happened in the study of American history over the last century. It was Winston Churchill who is credited with saying, "History is written by the victors," and for a long time, that was the predominant philosophy in history textbooks. Take, for instance, the representations of Native Americans. For decades, they were depicted as savages, and the American westward expansion was viewed as heroic and noble (i.e. "manifest destiny"). Those accounts of history portray the perspective of the white people who lived during that time, but more recently, we have come to value different accounts of history that include the perspectives of Native Americans, and so we are more critical of the treatment that they suffered at the hands of white settlers. We place much more value in understanding history from multiple angles, and we understand that in writing a history textbook, there is no absolute "truth," but only an examination of multiple points of view on historical events. Of course, not all points of view are equally tenable; some historical perspectives are more supportable than others by archaeological evidence and historical artifacts.

If we understand a text as an author's voice, the key distinction between a "research paper" and a bibliographic essay becomes much clearer. The goal of a bibliographic essay are to let the authors' voices speak in the paper and for the authors to metaphorically enter into a conversation with one another, agreeing on certain points and disagreeing on others. Instead of using an author's words to support your assertions, you set up the authors' voices to communicate with each other and debate the topic.

Assignment 3

For this assignment, you will write a 7 - 10 page essay (1,750 - 2,500 words) to inform your readers about the variety of viewpoints related to the topic you choose to write about (e.g. anti-aging, environmentalism, poverty in America, Islam in America, or whatever topic you choose and that your instructor has approved). You will also need to identify a specific audience for your essay.

The purpose of a bibliographic essay is *not* to take a side in a debate but to explore as many *different* sides of the issue as you can. In other words, your essay should answer the question, "What *are* the issues relevant to the topic I am writing about?"

Your essay should draw on 8 - 12 credible sources, no more than two of which should be web sites (and any web sites used must meet the standards of credibility as presented in the Widener University Library's Online Tutorial at

http://www3.widener.edu/Academics/Libraries/Wolfgram_Memorial_Library/Evaluate_Web_Pages/659/

No more than 10% of your essay should consist of quotes from your sources. Most of the essay should consist of summaries and paraphrases of your source material, as well as your own ideas.

Your essay should have 1" margins all around, using a 12-point font. Your instructor will provide you with additional formatting instructions.

Choosing a Topic

Because you now understand several of the important features of a bibliographic essay, let's return to an earlier analogy that will help you fully conceptualize your task in writing this essay. You can think of your bibliographic essay as a recreation of an "ongoing discussion" (Hjortshoj 155), as "a conversation, using what others say (or might say) as a launching pad or sounding board for your own ideas" (Graff and Birkenstein 3). To write a successful essay, you have to choose a good conversation to recreate.

There are innumerable ongoing "discussions" about our human existence, cultural identities, social responsibilities, and so on. These discussions range from the serious to the mundane, but one thing ties them all together: many different people weigh in on these discussions, keeping debate alive by adding their voices through writing and speaking in public forums and in private with their friends and families. Your instructor will help you identify current "discussions" that are appropriate for a 7 - 10 page bibliographic essay.

Exercise 15

Respond in writing to the following questions. Your instructor may ask you to hand in your responses.

A. Watch the nightly national news at 6:30 p.m. on NBC, ABC, or CBS. What news stories spark your interest? Why? What stories did you not like or understand?

B. Go to the Park Library and read through a copy of one of the weekly American newsmagazines (*Newsweek, U.S. News and World Report,* or *Time*). What major stories are being covered in the national news? International news? What editorials spark your interest? Write a brief summary of the most interesting article you come across, then write a paragraph about why it interests you.

C. Read a current issue of *CM Life.* What campus issues do its editors view as important? Are these the same issues that are important to you? Talk with your roommates or other students and generate a list of the most pressing issues to you as current CMU students.

D. Call your parents, grandparents, an aunt, or an uncle. Ask them about their biggest personal and/or societal concerns. Are these concerns different from your own? Are there common bonds between your concerns? Write a paragraph analyzing these similarities and differences.

Sample Topic 1: Poverty in America

In the 1930s, as part of his New Deal to pull America out of the Great Depression, President Franklin Roosevelt first established a federal minimum wage. In the years since, as the cost of living has gone up, the minimum wage has also been raised. In 2007, the federal minimum wage was $5.85 per hour; in July 2008, it was raised to $6.55; and in July 2009 it will be raised to $7.25. Some states have even instituted their own minimum wages above the federal standard as a means of trying to ensure that people who work for a living are able to provide for their own and their families' basic needs. Currently, the minimum wage in Michigan is $7.15.

A lot of people are concerned that the issues of wages, work, and poverty have taken a backseat in today's public discourse to worries about terrorism; however, the tremendous increase in oil and gas prices has shifted the focus a bit. To investigate this issue, we will watch an episode of the television series *30 Days* and read several sources that provide perspectives on poverty. Before your opinions are colored by these sources, however, take some time to complete Exercise 16.

Exercise 16

Respond to the following questions in writing. Your instructor may ask you to hand in your responses.

    A. Do you think poverty is a problem in America today? Why or why not?

    B. Do you think that poverty stems from being too lazy to work, or that there are other factors involved? Explain.

    C. What was your family's financial situation while you were growing up? Did you struggle to make ends meet? Were you comfortable? Did you have everything you could ever wish for? How do you think your personal financial history colors your perspective on poverty in America today?

    D. Go online and look up some photographs of the victims of Hurricane Katrina, both right after the storm and more current photos. What do you feel when you look at them?

30 Days, "Minimum Wage" Episode

Following the success of his documentary *Super Size Me*, in which he documented the changes he underwent living on a steady diet of McDonald's for 30 days, Morgan Spurlock developed a television series for the FX network called, not surprisingly, *30 Days*. The concept is that each hour-long episode follows a person for 30 days as he or she lives in a situation that makes him or her uncomfortable. Morgan Spurlock and his fiancé, Alex, did the first episode themselves, heading to Columbus, Ohio for a month to live on minimum wage. As you watch this episode, you should take notes on what you see. Use the following outline as a guide (you fill in the blanks).

    1. The rules of living on minimum wage
    2. DAY 1: $356 in the "bank"
    3. DAY 2: Finding jobs
    4. DAY 3: First day of work
    5. DAY 4: Ant infestation
    6. DAY 5: Shopping
    7. DAY 9: Health care
    8. DAY 10: Health care
    9. DAY 11: Emergency care

10. DAY 15:
11. DAY 17:
12. DAY 18:
13. DAY 19:
14. DAY 23: Children's arrival
15. DAY 25: Alex's 30th birthday
16. DAY 26–DAY 28:
17. DAY 29: Hospital bills
18. DAY 30: The final tally

Exercise 17

Read the two essays about poverty in Chapter 6, as well as the Anna Quindlen essay about poverty (on Blackboard), and respond in writing to the following questions. Your instructor may ask you to hand in your responses.

A. How have your opinions on poverty changed as a result of watching the *30 Days* episode and reading the essays?

B. Both Anna Quindlen and John Dart touch on the moral obligations of the affluent toward the poor. Find the passages that specifically relate to that theme. What do *you* think about what Quindlen and Dart have to say?

C. Several of these sources touch on the issue of minimum wage. What are the points of debate you can recognize in the discussion of whether to raise minimum wage? What do you think should be done? Who do you agree with, and why? Who do you disagree with, and why?

Sample Topic 2: Image, Beauty, and Aging in America

It is impossible to turn on the television or pick up a magazine or newspaper without two things happening: (1) you will be bombarded with images of beautiful, young people wearing clothes and participating in activities that you too are supposed to want to wear and do, and (2) you will find many people talking and writing about the effect these images have on individuals and our society.

Most people would agree that American culture is obsessed with youth and beauty. More and more people report being discontent with the way they look, and they take drastic measures to hang on to their youth or change their appearance in search of happiness. You will watch an episode of *30 Days* and an episode of the Showtime series *Penn and Teller: Bullshit!* and read several articles that present perspectives on our fixation on chasing the "fountain of youth." Before your views are colored by these sources, however, take some time to complete Exercise 18.

Exercise 18

Respond in writing to the following questions. Your instructor may ask you to hand in your responses.

A. Have you had any personal experience with body image struggles? Describe how you felt or feel. (If you don't feel comfortable answering this question about yourself, you may write about the experience of someone you know, e.g. a friend, a sibling.)

B. Do you know people who try to hang on to their youth? How does this desire manifest itself (e.g. in the person's appearance, choice of activities, use of language, and so forth)?

C. What evidence do you see around you of our culture's fixation on youth and beauty?

D. Do you think there are legitimate reasons for people to be worried about holding on to their youth? How does our society feel about the middle-aged and elderly? Are there real personal and economic drawbacks to looking your age?

---

30 Days, "Anti-Aging" Episode

In this episode of *30 Days,* 34-year-old Scott Bridges adopts an anti-aging regimen in an effort to counteract years of eating poorly and not taking care of himself. As you watch, take notes, using the following outline as a guide (you fill in the blanks).

1. Preliminary activities
2. Dr. Alan Miles, board-certified anti-aging doctor
3. Dr. Bill Pullen: possible long-term complications
4. Scott's sperm count
5. Scott's rules
6. DAY 1:
7. DAY 3:
8. DAY 4:
9. DAY 6:
10. DAY 9:
11. DAY 10:
12. DAY 12:
13. DAY 13:
14. DAY 14:
15. DAY 15:
16. DAY 18:
17. DAY 20:
18. DAY 21:
19. DAY 22:

Penn and Teller: Bullshit!, "Fountain of Youth" Episode

Penn and Teller's approach to their show is very different from Morgan Spurlock's. Penn and Teller are not really interested in being "fair and balanced" about anything; the title of their show is *Bullshit!* because their mission is to point out rationalizations and stupidity when they see it. They use a generous amount of swearing and pointed humor, but they get their point across. In this episode, their goal is to shed light on all the ridiculous decisions and actions of people chasing the "fountain of youth." Take notes using the following outline as a guide.

1. Penn and Teller's introduction
2. Los Angeles Botox party
3. Dr. David Rahimi, Forever Young, Los Angeles ($900 for a Botox treatment)
4. Dr. Renee Garfinkel, clinical psychologist at George Washington University
5. Richard Lynette, reporter and columnist, *Advertising Age* magazine
6. Paula Begone, consumer advocate and author of *Don't Go to the Cosmetics Counter Without Me*
7. Cindy Jackson
8. Dr. Rod Rourke, President, American Society of Plastic Surgeons
9. Dean Parmalo, 6 lbs of vegetables every day; has osteoporosis at age 37 and has lost sex drive
10. Dr. Dean Adell, medical journalist
11. Dr. Ron Kennedy, practices anti-aging medicine in southern California
12. Professor S. J. Oshanski, School of Public Health at University of Illinois, Chicago
13. Dr. Edward Schneider, Dean of University of Southern California
14. Miles Kendall

Exercise 19

Reread the essays about image and beauty in Chapter 6. Respond in writing to the following questions. Your instructor may ask you to hand in your responses.

A. How has watching and reading these sources changed your point of view on issues related to image, beauty, and aging?

B. How does Carl Elliot feel about shows like *The Swan* and about plastic surgery? Is he critical of these aspects of American society, or does he accept them? Point to textual evidence to support your opinion.

C. What do you think is the responsibility of modern medicine? Is it just as important to pursue advances in anti-aging as it is to pursue advances in other branches of medicine? Compare and contrast your viewpoint to what the authors and filmmakers in the sources have to say.

D. What do you think Thomas Withers would say to young men like Scott or to young women who seek plastic surgery?

Sample Topic 3: Environmental Concerns in America

Global warming, deforestation, pollution, and overdevelopment: one day, we hear these are serious problems, but then the next we are told they are not. And, more often, amid the worries over terrorism, job loss, health care, and others, environmental concerns fade into the background of public discourse. But, if we ignore these issues for too long and deplete our planet's resources too far, will we even need to be concerned about anything else?

What can just one person do? Is recycling and conserving fuel enough, or do we all need to take more drastic measures and make major lifestyle changes to save the environment? These are some of the issues explored in this unit, where you will watch an episode of *30 Days* and *Penn and Teller: Bullshit!,* as well as read some articles dealing with environmental issues. But before you are influenced by their opinions, take a moment to answer the following questions.

Exercise 20

Respond in writing to the following questions. Your instructor may ask you to hand in your responses.

A. What concerns do you have about the environment?

B. Have you ever considered giving up meat in your diet? Why or why not?

C. Describe the changes that have happened to the landscape in your hometown since you were a small child.

D. What do you think is your personal responsibility in preserving the environment?

E. What do you believe is society's or the government's responsibility in preserving the environment?

30 Days: "Off the Grid" Episode

In this episode of *30 Days,* Morgan Spurlock sends two born-and-bred New Yorkers, Vito and Johari, to Missouri, where they will live on an off-the-grid farm for one month. The farm is completely self-sufficient, generating its own energy, growing its own food, and disposing of its own waste. As you watch, take notes using the following outline as a guide (you fill in the blanks).

1. Introduction: the ecological footprint
2. The rules
3. DAY 1: Kirksville, Missouri
4. DAY 3:
5. DAY 5:
6. DAY 6:
7. DAY 10:
8. DAY 13:
9. DAY 15:
10. DAY 17:

11. DAY 20:
12. DAY 23:
13. DAY 25:
14. DAY 26:
15. DAY 27:
16. DAY 28:
17. DAY 30:

Penn and Teller: Bullshit! "Environmental Hysteria" Episode

As you watch this episode of *Penn and Teller: Bullshit!*, take notes using the following outline.

1. 1971: first Earth Day
2. Washington, D.C., environmental march
3. Kate Lowe, organizer for Rainforest Action Network
4. Ross Gelbspan, environmental journalist
5. Patrick Moore, ecologist and lifelong environmentalist; founding member of Greenpeace
6. Penn: couching socialism or anti-corporationism in environmentalism is bullshit
7. Penn and Teller's undercover agent goes around to see if people will sign a petition to ban "di-hydrogen monoxide," or H_2O (i.e. water).
8. Bjorn Lumborg, author of *The Skeptical Environmentalist*
9. Back to Ross Gelbspan
10. Jerry Taylor, Director of Natural Resource Studies, Cato Institute, a libertarian think-tank in Washington, D.C.
11. Is passion supposed to replace common sense?
12. Back to Patrick Moore
13. Julia Butterfly Hill
14. Back to Patrick Moore
15. Nina Facion, Vice President of Species Conservation, Defenders of Wildlife

Exercise 21

Read the essay on environmental concerns in Chapter 6, as well as the Anna Quindlen essay about the environment (on Blackboard) . Also, reread Herscovici's article, "Where's the Beef?" as well as the other article about vegetarianism on Blackboard that you compared with Herscovici's article in Chapter 3. Then, respond in writing to the following questions. Your instructor may ask you to hand in your responses.

A. How has watching and reading these sources changed your perspective about environmental concerns?

B. Divide the various environmental concerns highlighted in all these sources into categories and describe and provide examples for each category. Before you watched and read the sources, which of the categories would you have considered most serious? Did your opinion change after considering the sources?

C. Obviously, Penn and Teller present a far different point of view on the seriousness of environmental issues than some of the other sources (although it is important to recognize that Penn and Teller do not address overdevelopment). Which sources do you consider most credible? Why?

D. After reading and watching these sources, what environmental concerns would you be most interested in learning more about? Why?

Identifying a Thesis for Your Essay

As you know, all writing has to have a point, a thesis. Diana Hacker has provided an apt definition: "Thesis statements take a stand on a debatable issue—an issue about which intelligent, well-meaning people might disagree" (114). Instructors usually require a thesis statement at the beginning of an essay. However, just because the thesis goes at the beginning of the *paper,* that doesn't mean you should narrow in on a thesis at the beginning of your writing *process,* at least not if you're conducting credible research and writing a credible paper.

The challenge of synthesis is to wait to develop a thesis until the *end* of your research and prewriting process. The bonus, though, is that if you can hold off your natural urge to commit to a thesis early, the thesis will nearly write itself! Through your research, you should be noticing the ways in which authors agree and disagree. When those points of agreement and disagreement come up, stated in various ways, in several sources, you should be able to pin down the *major points of debate* within your overall topic. If you can write down those major points of debate in your own words, you should be able to craft them into a thesis for your own essay, something other than a simple opinion statement about who is "right" and who is "wrong."

Your thesis should reflect those major points of debate. For example, the thesis to Steve's high school essay was "The death penalty should be eliminated nationwide." Although that's a perfectly acceptable policy claim for an argument paper, it's not an acceptable thesis for a bibliographic essay, because it's one-sided; however, revising it to "There are many complex issues involved in the death penalty debate" is *not* the solution. That revision would be considered a "duh" thesis; who is going to disagree that there are complex issues involved in the death penalty debate? Similarly, a thesis like "There are many strong arguments for and against the death penalty" is equally unacceptable.

The thesis for your bibliographic essay may work in your opinion on the issue (without any first-person language—your teacher does *not* want to see any statements like "I think" or "I believe" creep into your thesis) while at the same time acknowledging that there are major points of debate. Steve's revised thesis for his English 101 essay makes a clear, debatable thesis: "Although there are many strong reasons capital punishment should be eliminated, there are many dissenting opinions on how to best punish serious criminal offenders." That thesis demonstrates that Steve has done enough research to understand the major points of the death penalty debate, and it sets him up to make a detailed, organized examination of those points. He is *not* arguing for or against capital punishment.

Use Figure 5 (which is also available on Blackboard) to help you analyze and synthesize information from your sources. This process will help you develop your thesis.

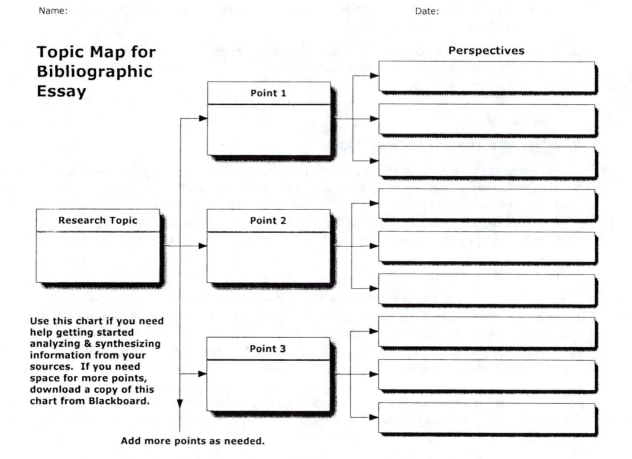

Figure 5: Topic Map for Bibliographic Essay

Organizing Your Essay

Once you have chosen an appropriate topic for your essay, found a variety of credible sources, and figured out what major points of debate exist among those sources, the question still remains about how best to *synthesize* those sources. The answer lies in remembering the metaphor of the "ongoing discussion." If you sit down to have a conversation with a friend, you don't say, "Okay, I'm going to talk for ten minutes, then you can talk for ten minutes, and then we'll be done." A conversation is about give and take, back and forth. Your essay should be organized with that same idea in mind. If you place your sources into a "pro" category and a "con" category, and then just have two sections to your essay that list "pro" views and then "con" views, you have *not* recreated a conversation. You must divide your paper into sections based on the *points of debate,* and let several "pro" and "con" sources weigh in on each point before moving onto a new point and repeating the same process. (This is called the *point-to-point* organizational structure and is useful for many types of writing, e.g. comparison/contrast essays, yardstick reports, and so on.)

By way of example, consider how Penn and Teller organize the episodes of *Bullshit!* The same expert might pop up three or four times in one episode, depending on how different parts of his or her interview pertain to different *points* Penn and Teller want to make about the overall topic. In that way, each episode of *Bullshit!* is a synthesis. Instead of just letting their experts do a long monologue, Penn and Teller use different opinions when they are relevant to different sections of the episode.

Another way Penn and Teller can help you understand the organization of your essay is in the *connections* they make between the interviews with the experts. In your essay, you need to do the same thing. If you don't make those connections, your essay will be nothing more than quotes and paraphrases from your sources strung together—and who wants to read that? Anyone could go find the sources you used and read the sources themselves. Your challenge is to make unique connections that make *your essay* worth reading, connections that help readers consider your topic in a way that they wouldn't if they just read your sources alone.

These connections (or transitions, if you are more familiar with that term), serve two functions. The first is to present your ideas, but in a way that is considerably more subtle than Penn and Teller. Simple sentences like "However, Smith's argument is clearly flawed, as Lisa Jones points out in her [...]" definitely show the way you feel about your topic, but without using weak constructions like "I believe." The phrase "clearly flawed" indicates that you think Smith is wrong, and you support your opinion with a part of Jones's source.

The second function of these connections is to help signal to your reader that you are introducing a new point of view. In an essay that requires the steady switching of "voices," just like a conversation, it is especially important that you help your reader follow along with simple words and phrases. Keeping track of who agrees or disagrees with whom is easy for you, because you have done all the necessary background reading. Do not lose sight of the fact that it will *not* be clear to your readers unless you use transitions. On the following page is a list of sample transitions (although it by no means includes all possible transitions).

A final important point to mention in organizing your essay relates to appropriate signal phrases. As noted in Chapter 1, signal phrases are the best way to introduce a quote or paraphrase because they *signal* to the reader where the information comes from. In a bibliographic essay, this is particularly important. Because you are recreating a conversation, it is only polite to introduce an author to your reader before you let the author "speak" in your essay—this is one way you establish credibility with your reader.

People like to know where information comes from, so you need to write signal phrases that give your reader some basic information about the author. What is his or her profession and credentials? What is the title of the article or book he or she wrote? What qualifies this author as a credible source on your topic? There is no magic formula for signal phrases, so you have to consider what information *you* would want to know if you were reading your essay. Once you have adequately introduced an author, it is appropriate to simply refer to him or her by last name throughout the rest of your essay.

Your instructor will also review how to avoid plagiarism by citing your sources using one of several documentation formats (e.g. APA, MLA, or Chicago). Citation is covered in most grammar and style handbooks, and your instructor will likely assign some citation practice activities.

COMPARISON TRANSITIONS	CONTRAST TRANSITIONS	ILLUSTRATIVE TRANSITIONS
Along the same lines,	But	For example,
In the same way,	However,	For instance,
Likewise,	Yet,	Specifically,
Similarly,	In contrast,	As an illustration,
Also,	Otherwise,	In particular,
Another	Still,	To illustrate,
In addition,	On the contrary,	To exemplify,
Moreover,	On the other hand,	To explain,
Furthermore,	Nonetheless,	…, such as…
	Nevertheless,	
	Conversely,	
	Despite	
	Whereas	
	Unlike	
	Although	
	In spite of	
	On the opposite side,	
	Even though	
	Regardless.	
	While	

Exercise 22

Read the sample bibliographic essays in Chapter 6, and respond in writing to the following questions. Your instructor may ask you to hand in your responses.

A. **Audience and Purpose:** Who do you think is the intended audience for each essay? Why do you think so?

B. **The Topic:** Is the topic of each essay sufficiently focused? Too narrow? Too broad?

C. **The Thesis:** Where is the thesis statement located in each essay? Is it clear? Appropriate? Placed effectively within the paper?

D. **Objectivity:** Do the authors of each essay avoid using words and phrases that expose the author's own biases? Are words and phrases used that suggest each author is fair and reasonable in presenting the various perspectives on the topic?

E. **Organization:** Does each essay have a clear beginning, middle, and end (i.e. an introduction, body, and conclusion)? Is the body of each essay organized around the *points of debate*? Are the points of debate organized in a way that makes sense? Or do the organizational patterns of any of the essays seem haphazard and not very well conceived?

F. **Comprehensiveness and Relevance:** Have the authors of each essay addressed all the major points relevant to the debate over the topic? Are all the points that are addressed directly relevant to the debate? Do any points seem irrelevant, trivial, or tangential?

G. **Handling of Source Material:** Have the authors of each essay effectively used signal phrases to introduce quotations and paraphrases from their sources? Are sources correctly and consistently cited using only *one* citation format (MLA, APA, or perhaps Chicago)?

H. **Readability and Appropriateness:** Are the authors' ideas expressed clearly and concisely? Are the style and tone of each essay appropriate for the intended audience and the purpose? Are the essays edited well?

 Peer Revision Workshop Questions for Assignment 3

Read your classmate's draft once without making any comments. Then, read it a second time and respond in writing to the following questions. Attach your written responses to the author's draft.

Feel free to write your comments (e.g., praise, criticism, suggestions) directly on the draft and/or on this checklist. Keep in mind the purpose of this assignment.

Audience and Purpose: Who is the intended audience for the author's paper? If you can't tell, ask the author to tell you. Is the purpose of the paper clear?

The Topic: Is it sufficiently focused? Too narrow? Too broad? (Hint: As you continue to read the paper, if you feel that the presentation of the points of the debate seems superficial or too obvious—i.e. if you have a "duh!" reaction—then the topic is probably too broad; either that or the author hasn't done a good job of researching the topic.)

The Thesis: Is it clear? Appropriate? Placed effectively within the paper? (Hint: A good place is at the end of the introduction, before the body begins. In some cases, however, the thesis might be effectively placed at the beginning of the essay, even serving as the first sentence—such placement, however, is more typical of business—writing than academic writing.)

Objectivity: Does the author avoid using words and phrases that expose the author's own bias? Are words and phrases used that suggest the author is fair and reasonable in presenting the various perspectives on the topic? (Recall that the purpose of this assignment is *not* for the author to argue a specific position but to present—as fairly and objectively as possible—many different views of the topic. It's OK if, at the *end* of the paper, the author states which view(s) he or she finds most reasonable and why.

Organization: Does the paper have a clear beginning, middle, and end (i.e. an introduction, body, and conclusion)? Is the body of the paper organized around the *points of debate?* Are the points of debate organized in a way that makes sense? Or does the organizational pattern seem haphazard and not very well conceived?

Comprehensiveness and Relevance: Has the author addressed all the major points relevant to the debate about this topic? Are all the points that are addressed directly relevant to the debate? Do any points seem irrelevant, trivial, or tangential?

Handling of Source Material: Has the author effectively used signal phrases to introduce quotations and paraphrases from his or her sources? Are sources correctly and consistently cited using only *one* citation format (MLA, APA, or perhaps Chicago)?

Readability and Appropriateness: Are the author's ideas expressed clearly and concisely? Are the style and tone of the paper appropriate for the intended audience and the purpose? Is the paper edited well? (At this point, the draft may not be well-edited, so remind the author to proofread and edit carefully before handing in the paper to your instructor by the due date.)

Final Thoughts

In this chapter, you have developed many important skills that will carry over into all the writing you will do in college. When you are assigned small essays or large-scale research projects in your future classes, try to remember the lessons of the informative essay:

- Recreate conversations or debates over issues by researching multiple sides.

- Use detailed signal phrases to introduce sources and establish their credibility (and yours).

- Focus on the points of debate.

- Present multiple sides of the debate without shortchanging viewpoints that oppose yours.

In English 201, you will learn to write research-based argument essays in which you *do* take a side.

Works Cited for Chapter 4

30 Days. "Anti-Aging." Writ. Penn Jillette Teller, Star Price, John McLaughlin, Jon Hotchkiss, Emma Webster, Jonathan Taylor, David Wechter, Michael Goudeau. Dir. Star Price. FX Network. 2005.

---. "Minimum Wage." Writ. Penn Jillette Teller, Star Price, John McLaughlin, Jon Hotchkiss, Emma Webster, Jonathan Taylor, David Wechter, Michael Goudeau. Dir. Star Price. FX Network. 2005.

---. "Off the Grid." Writ. Penn Jillette Teller, Star Price, John McLaughlin, Jon Hotchkiss, Emma

Booth, Wayne C., Gregory G. Colomb, and Joseph M. Williams. *The Craft of Research.* 3rd ed. Chicago: U of Chicago P.

Graff, Gerald, and Cathy Birkenstein. *They Say/I Say.* New York: W.W. Norton and Company, 2006.

Hacker, Diana. *A Pocket Style Manual.* 4th ed. Boston: Bedford/St. Martin's, 2004.

Hjortshoj, Keith. *The Transition to College Writing.* Boston: Bedford/St. Martin's, 2001.

Kantz, Margaret. "Helping Students Use Textual Sources Persuasively." *The Allyn and Bacon Sourcebook for College Writing Teachers*. 2nd ed. James C. McDonald, ed. Boston: Allyn and Bacon, 2000.

Penn and Teller: Bullshit! "Environmental Hysteria." Prod. Mark Wolper and Star Price. Showtime. 2002.

---. "Fountain of Youth." Prod. Mark Wolper and Star Price. Showtime. 2003.

Webster, Jonathan Taylor, David Wechter, Michael Goudeau. Dir. Star Price. FX Network. 2005.

The Oxford American Desk Dictionary and Thesaurus. 2nd ed. Oxford and London: Oxford University Press, 2001.

Chapter 5: Reflecting on Your Literacy

Why Write a Literacy Autobiography?

In "The Day Language Came into My Life," Helen Keller chronicles the amazing transformation that took place when Annie Sullivan—who was Keller's teacher, mentor, and friend—finally penetrated and opened the deaf, dumb, and mute world in which Helen had been imprisoned:

> I stood still, my whole attention fixed upon the motions of [Annie's] fingers. Suddenly I felt a misty consciousness as of something forgotten—a thrill of returning thought; and somehow the mystery of language was revealed to me. I knew then that "w-a-t-e-r" meant the wonderful cool something that was flowing over my hand. The living word awakened my soul, gave it light, hope, joy, set it free. [...] I left the well-house eager to learn. Everything had a name, and each name gave birth to a new thought. As we returned to the house, every object which I touched seemed to quiver with life. That was because I saw everything with the strange, new sight that had come to me. (112–113)

Unlike Keller, most people do not remember even the day, let alone the moment, that language came into their lives, and it is possible to spend an entire lifetime reading, writing, and speaking (the most common literacy activities) not being truly cognizant of them because literacy is, on one level, transparent. It is just *there*, not unlike the air we breathe, and yet language—both language development and language use—is more than *merely there*. Put simply, you are a literate person because you are able to use language. Through language, we understand the world around us; we create meaning, convey ideas, and identify ourselves among others. In other words, literacy is a rich and complex phenomenon that speaks volumes about who we are and what we value, both as individuals and as group members. In short, our literacy development and practices are worthy of serious examination, reflection, and study.

Countless literacy studies exist in the academic world. An excellent example is Mina Shaughnessy's *Errors and Expectations,* a groundbreaking study of the writing processes and products of first-year students at the City University of New York during the open-admissions policy of the 1970s. Or consider Andrea Lunsford's and Lisa Ede's *Singular Texts/Plural Authors,* a landmark study of collaborative writing practices for literally hundreds of businesspeople in seven professional associations.

On the other hand, other literacy studies extend far beyond college and university borders. Perhaps the best known are the studies by Deborah Tannen, a linguist at Georgetown University, whose study of everyday conversations at home, at work, and at play have resulted in several best-selling books: *You're Wearing That?: Understanding Mothers and Daughters in Conversation; You Just Don't Understand: Women and Men in Conversation; That's Not What I Meant: How Conversational Style Makes or Breaks Professional Relationships;* and *The Argument Culture: Moving from Debate to Dialogue.* Although nonfiction, these books are "good reads" by virtually anyone's standards, because they are written in an entertaining and persuasive way and because they help us better understand ourselves and our relationships with others, both in our personal and professional lives.

Deborah Brandt has been studying literacy for two decades, and one of her earliest publications focuses on interviews she conducted in the early 1990s with 40 Wisconsin residents, varying in age, ethnicity, socioeconomic class, and so on. Brandt was interested in what they remembered about their literacy development: "the interviews focused on what people could remember about learning to read and write across their lifetimes, particularly the occasions, people, materials, and motivations involved in the processes. I also asked about the uses and purposes of literacy at various stages of people's lives" (461).

As the Shaughnessy, Lunsford and Ede, Tannen, and Brandt examples suggest, it is fairly common to conduct large-scale literacy studies, but it is equally probable and productive to assess the literacy practices of smaller groups and even individuals within groups. For example, consider the work of Speed B. Leas, a national expert on conflict management in both small and large church cultures across the United States. As a senior consultant at The Alban Institute, Leas wrote *Discover Your Conflict Management Style*, a book that helps individuals analyze their literacy practices as they relate to conflict management. To this end, Leas claims that "conflict is a part of everyone's life; we can't eliminate it. Nor would we necessarily want to—for new insights and growth can emerge from well-managed conflict" (iii). To help individuals productively manage conflicts, Leas identifies and describes six common strategies—persuading, compelling, avoiding and accommodating, collaborating, negotiating, and/or supporting (4)—and he explains when and why these literacy practices tend to work—or not. Next, he offers "the conflict inventory" (35) to help readers analyze their own literacy practices in conflict situations, so that they can become more aware of their own tendencies and, in turn, be better equipped to resolve conflicts.

Conflict management or self-improvement, however, is not the only topic of small scale or individual literacy studies or reflections. Consider the following examples of informal literacy studies, grouped in the potentially overlapping categories of reading, writing, and speaking:

Reading

- A history major takes pleasure in tracing her academic interests to a childhood love of the *Little House* books.

- Chat buddies swap family stories on the Internet; based on the stories they read, the buddies begin to learn the values of their friends' families and how they intersect with their own family's values.

- A recently engaged couple is creating a wedding invitation. To get ideas, the couple analyzes their parents' and married friends' wedding invitations.

Writing

- A new English teacher analyzes why his students' homecoming and prom narratives are so loathsome to him.

- A high school senior finds her 6th grade diary and remembers an adolescent obsession with babysitting and boys.

- A business communication professor urges students to reconsider writing overly informal emails to faculty members.

Speaking

- A man analyzes his grandmother's repetitive speech patterns to determine whether she is lonely, forgetful, or on the verge of developing Alzheimer's disease.

- A recent college graduate learns that regional speech patterns really do exist when he moves from Michigan to Indiana.

- A parent tries to explain to an adolescent daughter why she should not refer to herself as "a chick," and the daughter explains why it's "totally okay" for her and her friends to do so.

For the fourth assignment, you will reflect on, analyze, and draw conclusions about your own literacy. As the previous examples suggest, you will most likely select a topic related to a reading, writing, or speaking activity.

Exercise 23

To begin this assignment, brainstorm a list of at least twenty different kinds of literacy activities in each of three overlapping categories: *reading, writing,* and *speaking.* Be prepared to discuss your list in class. Your instructor may ask you to hand in your list.

Exercise 24

Read Deborah Brandt's article "Remembering Writing, Remembering Reading," which is on Blackboard, and respond to the following questions in writing. Your instructor may ask you to hand in your responses.

A. Where in the essay does Brandt state the purpose of *the interviews* she conducted? Quote the passage and cite the specific page number.

B. Where in the essay does Brandt state the purpose of *the essay* she has written about the interviews she conducted? Quote the passage and cite the specific page number.

C. Where does Brandt summarize the *major finding* of her research, i.e. where does she explain the major difference between respondents' memories of learning to read and learning to write? Quote the passage and cite the specific page number.

D. List five examples from Brandt's essay that she uses to illustrate the major finding of her research. Just paraphrase the examples and cite the specific page numbers.

Respond in writing to the following questions. Your instructor may ask you to hand in your responses.

A. Describe five papers that you remember writing in middle school or high school.

B. Identify the kinds of nonacademic writing you produce (e.g. at work, as a member of a club, at church, as a hobby).

C. Recall a time when you used a word or phrase at the wrong place or time. What happened? How did you know it was a mistake? What literacy conventions or norms did you violate?

D. Did you take a foreign language in high school? How did studying a foreign language help you better understand English?

E. Briefly describe three stories typically repeated at your house during holidays or annual events. What do the stories say about your family's values, assumptions, or lifestyle choices?

F. Consider the following statements: *By listening to me talk, anyone could tell that I'm a white, middle-class girl or a Californian transplant or an ex-Marine or a PK (preacher's kid) because we all sound alike.* Revise the statement to reflect one aspect of your own cultural background and then explain the conversational traits that support the claim.

G. Think about the ideological function of language—that is, how language upholds cultural values. When you hear phrases, such as "He plays soccer like a girl" or "That's so gay," what attitudes and assumptions are being upheld? What other examples can you think of that would be considered "loaded" language?

H. Etymology is the history of a word. Using the CMU library's access to the Oxford English Dictionary Online (see Virtual Reference Collection on Park Library's homepage), look up the etymology of an interesting word. What other words come from the same roots, and how does an understanding of the origin and development influence your literacy practices?

I. The English language is a living language, constantly growing and changing as millions of people use it daily. Think of words that have changed in their meaning as a result of people using the word in new and different ways. Have you ever adopted a word to mean something different than its common definition? How did that choice affect the way you communicated with others?

J. Words have a *denotation* (the dictionary definition) and a *connotation* (the feelings and images people associate with the word as a result of common cultural factors or personal experiences). Are there words that make you uncomfortable because of their connotation? Why? How does your discomfort affect your literacy development or practices?

Assignment 4

Write a 6 – 8 page essay (1,500 - 2,000 words) in which you do one of the following:

- Describe and analyze an event that shaped your literacy development, examining the effects of the event on your development as a literate person. OR

- Describe and analyze a literacy practice you participate in and how that practice makes you a part of a certain group or community. OR

- Describe your literacy history, i.e. in Brandt's words, the history of "what [you remember] about learning to read and write since childhood, particularly the occasions, people, materials, and motivations involved in the processes, as well as the uses and purposes of literacy at various stages of [your life]" (461).

Try to share with readers some *compelling* aspect of your literacy development or literacy practices. That aspect should be original and specific, and your perspective should be detailed, developed, and analytical. In other words, do not provide a "museum tour" of a great high school English class or a "bird's-eye view" of your elementary schooling just for the sake of narrating it, assignment by assignment or year by year. This autobiography should be more than just a good story—in it, you should reflect on and critically analyze your literacy experiences.

Your essay should be double-spaced with 1"margins all around, using a 12-point font. Your instructor will provide you with additional formatting instructions.

Writing the Rough Draft

Don't set out to write all 6 – 8 pages from start to finish in one or two sessions. Also, resist a common misconception: *I can either write a good paper that is short or a long one filled with BS.* As Deborah Tannen explains in *The Argument Culture,* this mutually exclusive, binary thinking is prevalent in American culture, but it obscures facts and restricts creative thinking. After all, isn't it possible that a third choice defies the short/good versus long/BS paper-length debate? The answer is "yes," and the third choice is to write a long paper that is also good. How is this goal accomplished? Part of the answer stems from good topic selection, but it is also possible to add length while simultaneously building substance and support using the following strategies (which are really just variations on the rhetorical strategies presented in Chapter 3!):

- A series of short examples
- An extended example
- A comparison
- An anecdote or story
- A logical extension
- A relevant quotation with an explanation
- A definition

Read the sample literacy autobiographies in Chapter 6, and respond in writing to the following questions. Your instructor may ask you to hand in your responses.

A. Is Dustin Fox's essay a development or a practice literacy autobiography, or does it combine elements of both? Point out specific passages that specifically analyze an aspect of Fox's literacy development and how his literacy practices define him as a member of a discourse community.

B. In Laura Grow's essay, what specific aspect of literacy does she explore? Does the essay more explore her literacy development or her literacy practices?

C. Which essay, Fox's or Grow's, do you relate to more? Why?

Peer Revision Workshop Questions for Assignment 4

Read your classmate's draft once without making any comments. Then, read it a second time and respond in writing to the following questions. Attach your written responses to the author's draft. Feel free to write your comments (e.g., praise, criticism, suggestions) directly on the draft and/or on this checklist. Keep in mind the purpose of this assignment.

Audience and Purpose

- Who is the intended audience for the author's paper? If you can't tell, ask the author.

- What is the author's purpose in this paper? Can you tell?

Content: Has the author followed the instructions and done *one* of the following?

- Described a specific event that has shaped his or her literacy development?

- Described the literacy or language practices of a specific group to which she or he belongs?

- Described the author's literacy history, i.e. in Brandt's words, the history of "what [the author] remembers about learning to read and write since childhood, particularly the occasions, people, materials, and motivations involved in the processes, as well as the uses and purposes of literacy at various stages of [his or her life]" (461).

Organization

- Is the paper well-organized overall? Is there a clear beginning, middle, and end?

- What about within individual paragraphs? Are there clear, nicely focused topic sentences at the beginning of each paragraph?

Writing Style

- Are the author's ideas expressed clearly and concisely?

- Has the author vividly portrayed the content by using plenty of descriptive language that engages the reader's senses?

- Are the style and tone of the paper appropriate for the intended audience and the purpose? (Remember, 2nd-person "you" should be used *only* to refer directly to the reader.)

- Has the author used stylistic and rhetorical strategies effectively, e.g. allusion, anecdote, metaphor or simile, example?

- Is the paper edited well?

Final Thoughts

The literacy autobiography is the fourth and final ENG 101 assignment. It should have given you a greater awareness of yourself as a writer and reader.

In the future, continue to pay attention to your own literacy practices and those of others. After all, language is a powerful force that gives individuals the ability to "construct reality." As Brockman points out, it can "build or break ... self-image[s]. It can reinforce or ruin professional relationships. It can enhance or eradicate public relations. It can promote or impede policies and programs. It can increase or annihilate *esprit de corps*" (2). With all of this in mind, please consider the following questions:

1. How do you use language to promote positive or negative change? What language builds relationships or silences others?

2. What can you do to foster literacy awareness and growth?

Works Cited for Chapter 5

Brandt, Deborah. "Remembering Writing, Remembering Reading." *College Composition and Communication* 45.4 (Dec. 1994): 459-79.

Brockman, Elizabeth. *The Blue Guide: Written Communication for Leaders in Law Enforcement.* Boston: Allyn & Bacon, 2007.

Keller, Helen. "The Day Language Came into My Life" in *The Prentice Hall Guide for College Writers.* Ed. S. Reid. Upper Saddle River NJ: Prentice Hall, 2003. 110-113

Leas, Speed B. *Discover Your Conflict Management Style.* Herndon VA: Alban Institute, 1997.

Lunsford, Andrea and Lisa Ede. *Singular Texts/Plural Authors: Perspectives on Collaborative Writing.* Carbondale, IL: Southern Illinois UP, 1990.

Shaughnessy, Mina. *Errors and Expectations: A Guide for the Teacher of Basic Writing.* New York: Oxford UP, 1977.

Tannen, Deborah. *That's Not What I Meant: How Conversational Style Makes or Breaks Professional Relationships.* New York: Ballantine Books, 1987.

____. *The Argument Culture: Moving from Debate to Dialogue.* New York: Ballantine, 1999.

____. *You Just Don't Understand: Women and Men in Conversation.* New York: Harper Paperbacks, 2001.

____. *You're Wearing That?: Understanding Mothers and Daughters in Conversation.* New York: Random House, 2006.

Chapter 6: Essays for Analysis

Exercise 2 Essays

I'm O.K., but You're Not

Robert Zoellner

The American novelist John Barth, in his early novel, *The Floating Opera*, remarks that ordinary, day-to-day life often presents us with embarrassingly obvious, totally unsubtle patterns of symbolism and meaning—life in the midst of death, innocence vindicated, youth versus age, etc.

The truth of Barth's insight was brought home to me recently while having breakfast in a lawn-bordered restaurant on College Avenue near the Colorado State University campus. I had asked to be seated in the smoking section of the restaurant—I have happily gone through three or four packs a day for the past 40 years.

As it happened, the hostess seated me—I was by myself—at a little two-person table on the dividing line between the smoking and non-smoking sections. Presently, a well-dressed couple of advanced years, his hair a magisterial white and hers an electric blue, were seated in the non-smoking section five feet away from me. It was apparent within a minute that my cigarette smoke was bugging them badly, and soon the husband leaned over and asked me if I would please stop smoking. As a chronic smokestack, I normally comply, out of simple courtesy, with such requests. Even an addict such as myself can quit for as long as 20 minutes.

But his manner was so self-righteous and peremptory—he reminded me of Lee Iacocca boasting about Chrysler—that the promptings of original sin, always a problem with me, took over. I quietly pointed out that I was in the smoking section—if only by five feet—and that that fact meant that I had met my social obligation to non-smokers. Besides, the idea of morning coffee without a cigarette was simply inconceivable to me—might as well ask me to vote Republican.

The two of them ate their eggs-over-easy in hurried and sullen silence, while I chain-smoked over my coffee. As well as be hung for a sheep as a lamb, I reasoned. Presently they got up, paid their bill, and stalked out in an ambiance of affronted righteousness and affluent propriety.

And this is where John Barth comes in. They had parked their car—a diesel Mercedes—where it could be seen from my table. And in the car, waiting impatiently, was a splendidly matched pair of pedigreed poodles, male and female.

Both dogs were clearly in extremis, and when the backdoor of the car was opened, they made for the restaurant lawn in considerable haste. Without ado (no pun intended), the male did a doo-doo that would have done credit to an animal twice his size, and finished off with a leisurely, ruminative wee-wee. The bitch of the pair, as might be expected of any well-brought-up female of Republican proclivities, confined herself to a modest wee-wee, fastidious, diffident, and quickly executed.

Having thus polluted the restaurant lawn, the four of them marshaled their collective dignity and drove off in a dense cloud of blue smoke—the lovely Mercedes was urgently in need of a valve-and-ring job, its emission sticker an obvious exercise in creative writing.

As I regretfully watched them go—after all, the four of them had made my day—it seemed to me that they were in something of a hurry, and I uncharitably wondered if the husband was not anxious to get home in order to light the first Fall fire in his moss-rock fireplace, or apply the Fall ration of chemical fertilizer to his doubtlessly impeccable lawn, thus adding another half-pound of particulates to the local atmosphere and another 10 pounds of nitrates and other poisons to the regional aquifers. But that, of course, is pure and unkindly speculation.

In any case, the point of this real-life vignette, as John Barth would insist, is obvious. The current controversy over public smoking in Fort Collins is a clear instance of selective virtue at work, coming under the rubric of, what I do is perfectly OK, but what you do is perfectly awful.

Lost Lives of Women

Amy Tan

When I first saw this photo as a child, I thought it was exotic and remote, of a faraway time and place, with people who had no connection to my American life. Look at their bound feet! Look at that funny lady with the plucked forehead!

The solemn little girl is, in fact, my mother. And leaning against the rock is my grandmother, Jingmei. "She called me Baobei," my mother told me. "It means Treasure."

The picture was taken in Hangzhou, and my mother believes the year was 1922, possibly spring or fall, judging by the clothes. At first glance, it appears the women are on a pleasure outing.

But see the white bands on their skirts? The white shoes? They are in mourning. My mother's grandmother, known to the others as Divong, "The Replacement Wife," has recently died. The women have come to this place, a Buddhist retreat, to perform yet another ceremony for Divong. Monks hired for the occasion have chanted the proper words. And the women and little girl have walked in circles clutching smoky sticks of incense. They knelt and prayed, then burned a huge pile of spirit money so that Divong might ascend to a higher position in her new world.

This is also a picture of secrets and tragedies, the reasons that warnings have been passed along in our family like heirlooms. Each of these women suffered a terrible fate, my mother said. And they were not peasant women but big city people, very modern. They went to dance halls and wore stylish clothes. They were supposed to be the lucky ones.

Look at the pretty woman with her finger on her cheek. She is my mother's second cousin, Nunu Aiyi, "Precious Auntie." You cannot see this, but Nunu Aiyi's entire face was scarred from smallpox. Lucky for her, a year or so after this picture was taken, she received marriage proposals from two families. She turned down a lawyer and married another man. Later she divorced her husband, a daring thing for a woman to do. But then, finding no means to support herself or her young daughter, Nunu eventually accepted the lawyer's second proposal, to become his number two concubine. "Where else could she go?" my mother asked. "Some people said she was lucky the lawyer still wanted her."

Now look at the small woman with a sour face. There's a reason that Jyou Ma, "Uncle's Wife," looks this way. Her husband, my great-uncle, often complained that his family had chosen an ugly woman for his wife. To show his displeasure, he often insulted

Jyou Ma's cooking. One time Great-Uncle tipped over a pot of boiling soup, which fell all over his niece's four-year-old neck and nearly killed her. My mother was the little niece, and she still has that soup scar on her neck. Great-Uncle's family eventually chose a pretty woman for his second wife. But the complaints about Jyou Ma's cooking did not stop.

Doomma, "Big Mother," is the regal-looking woman seated on a rock. (The woman with the plucked forehead, far left, is a servant, remembered only as someone who cleaned but did not cook.) Doomma was the daughter of my great-grandfather and Nu-pei, "The Original Wife." She was shunned by Divong, "The Replacement Wife," for being "too strong," and loved by Divong's daughter, my grandmother. Doomma's first daughter was born with a hunchback—a sign, some said, of Doomma's own crooked nature. Why else did she remarry, disobeying her family's orders to remain a widow forever? And why did Doomma later kill herself, using some mysterious means that caused her to die slowly over three days? "Doomma died the same way she lived," my mother said, "strong, suffering lots."

Jingmei, my own grandmother, lived only a few more years after this picture was taken. She was the widow of a poor scholar, a man who had the misfortune of dying from influenza when he was about to be appointed a vice-magistrate. In 1924 or so, a rich man, who liked to collect pretty women, raped my grandmother and thereby forced her into becoming one of his concubines. My grandmother, now an outcast, took her young daughter to live with her on an island outside of Shanghai. She left her son behind, to save his face. After she gave birth to another son she killed herself by swallowing raw opium buried in the New Year's rice cakes. The young daughter who wept at her deathbed was my mother.

At my grandmother's funeral, monks tied chains to my mother's ankles so she would not fly away with her mother's ghost. "I tried to take them off," my mother said. "I was her treasure. I was her life."

My mother could never talk about any of this, even with her closest friends. "Don't tell anyone," she once said to me. "People don't understand. A concubine was like some kind of prostitute. My mother was a good woman, high-class. She had no choice."

I told her I understood.

"How can you understand?" she said, suddenly angry. "You did not live in China then. You do not know what it's like to have no position in life. I was her daughter. We had no face! We belonged to nobody! This is a shame I can never push off my back." By the end of the outburst, she was crying.

On a recent trip with my mother to Beijing, I learned that my uncle found a way to push the shame off his back. He was the son my grandmother left behind. In 1936 he joined the Communist party—in large part, he told me, to overthrow the society that forced his mother into concubinage. He published a story about his mother. I told him I had written about my grandmother in a book of fiction. We agreed that my grandmother is the source of strength running through our family. My mother cried to hear this.

My mother believes my grandmother is also my muse, that she helps me write. "Does she still visit you often?" she asked while I was writing my second book. And then she added shyly, "Does she say anything about me?"

"Yes," I told her. "She has lots to say. I am writing it down."

This is the picture I see when I write. These are the secrets I was supposed to keep. These are the women who never let me forget why stories need to be told.

Exercise 5 Essay

Surviving a Year of Sleepless Nights

Jenny Hung

Now a high-school senior, I still remember my freshman year with a shudder; it was the year my friends and I joked about as the "Year of Sleepless Nights." It wasn't that I had contracted a rare sleeping disorder or suffered from a bad case of insomnia that particular year; in fact, nothing could have been further from the truth. I had done what many diligent students do: sacrifice precious sleep for the sake of academic success.

Don't get me wrong; my parents never mandated that I take all the honors classes I could gain admission to. No one told me to take three honors classes. No one, that is, except the little voice in my head that convinced me scholarly success was based upon the number of "H's" on my high-school transcript. The counselors cautioned me not to do it, students who had fallen into the trap before warned me against it and my parents just left it up to me. Through it all, I just smiled and reassured them, "Don't worry; I can handle it." The trouble was, I didn't have the slightest idea what lay ahead.

I soon found myself mired in work. For a person whose friends teased her about being a neat freak, I grew increasingly messy. My room and desk looked like my backpack had exploded. There was no time to talk to friends on the phone, not even on the weekends. Going to bed at midnight was a luxury, 1 a.m. was normal, 3 a.m. meant time to panic and 4 a.m. meant it was time to go to sleep defeated. Most days, I would shuffle clumsily from class to class with sleep-clouded eyes and nod off during classroom lectures. There was even a month in winter when I was so self-conscious of my raccoon eyes that I wore sunglasses at school.

My parents applauded my academic success but hardly knew the price I paid for it. I vividly remember one night when my mother couldn't fall asleep. She kept going to bed and getting up again. Every time I heard her get up, I'd turn off my light so she wouldn't catch me still awake. By 5 o'clock that morning, I was so sleepy that I didn't hear her footsteps as she shuffled down the hallway. When she saw the light under my door, she came in and demanded to know why I wasn't sleeping. That was when I knew I was defeated for the night. My mother frowned at me with concern, and I no longer had the strength or energy to resist the temptation to rest. I woke up two hours later and got dressed for school.

Despite the sleep-deprived state I constantly lived in, the A's kept coming home on my report card, and my homework was always turned in on time. I caught up on my sleep in what little spare time I could snatch on the weekends. I had created my own hell, and I was determined to endure until I could get myself out of it.

By the time my freshman year ended, I was rewarded for my hard work. My school held an academic assembly in May, and posters naming the top 10 students in each grade dangled from the ceiling. And there, on the top of the freshman list, I saw: "1.) Jenny Hung GPA: 4.43." The sight of my name on that list was gratifying after all the hard work I had poured into getting it up there, but it also made me think. Was that position really that important to me? Did I want to remember high school as nights without sleep and days of work? Sure, the weight of the medal felt good in my hand, but it didn't mean much. That I would remain at the top of that list was doubtful, and in the end, the paper of the poster was biodegradable. There can only be one valedictorian in each class, and that person usually has to work his fingers to the bone against fierce competition to claim that position. That life, I decided, was not for me.

When sophomore year came around, I chose my classes carefully. The honors classes didn't completely disappear from my transcript, but they weren't as plentiful as before. I found myself busy with all the extracurricular activities that began to fill up my days. My friends no longer thought of me as the outsider who slept through lunchtime gossip. I felt the joy of holding a yearbook I helped to create, and spent hours on the phone comforting a friend who had burst into tears over her dropping grades.

After all these experiences, I frown when I hear my classmates tell stories about their parents pressuring them to do well in school. Sometimes I wonder if their parents understand to what lengths their children go so they can sport bumper stickers on their cars proclaiming MY CHILD GOES TO HARVARD! If that's the case, they need to learn what my parents and I have learned: academic success means nothing if your heart isn't into earning it, and in the end, books will always fail to teach you as much as life itself.

Exercise 7, Reflection Set 1

Beauty: When the Other Dancer Is the Self

Alice Walker

It is a bright summer day in 1947. My father, a fat, funny man with beautiful eyes and a subversive wit, is trying to decide which of his eight children he will take with him to the county fair. My mother, of course, will not go. She is knocked out from getting us ready: I hold my neck stiff against the pressure of her knuckles as she hastily completes the braiding and then beribboning of my hair.

My father is the driver for the rich old white lady up the road. Her name is Miss Mey. She owns all the land for miles around, as well as the house in which we live. All I remember about her is that she once offered to pay my mother thirty-five cents for cleaning her house, raking up piles of her magnolia leaves, and washing her family's clothes, and that my mother—she of no money, eight children, and a chronic earache—refused it. But I do not think of this in 1947. I am two-and-a-half years old. I want to go everywhere my daddy goes. I am excited at the prospect of riding in a car. Someone has told me fairs are fun. That there is room in the car for only three of us doesn't faze me at all. Whirling happily in my starchy frock, showing off my biscuit polished patent leather shoes and lavender socks, tossing my head in a way that makes my ribbons bounce, I stand, hands on hips, before my father. "Take me, Daddy," I say with assurance, "I'm the prettiest!"

Later, it does not surprise me to find myself in Miss Mey's shiny black car, sharing the backseat with the other lucky ones. Does not surprise me that I thoroughly enjoy the fair. At home that night I tell all the unlucky ones about the merry-go-round, the man who eats live chickens, and the abundance of Teddy bears, until they say: that's enough, baby Alice. Shut up now, and go to sleep.

It is Easter Sunday, 1950. I am dressed in a green, flocked scalloped-hem dress (handmade by my adoring sister Ruth) that has its own smooth satin petticoat and tiny hot-pink roses tucked into each scallop. My shoes, new T-strap patent leather, again highly biscuit polished. I am six years old and have learned one of the longest Easter speeches to be heard in church that day, totally unlike the speech I said when I was two: "Easter lilies/ pure and white/ blossom in/ the morning light." When I rise to give my speech I do so on a great wave of love and pride and expectation. People in the church stop rustling their new crinolines. They seem to hold their breath. I can tell they admire my dress, but it is my spirit, bordering on sassiness (womanishness), they secretly applaud.

"That girl's a little *mess*," they whisper to each other, pleased.

Naturally I say my speech without stammer or pause, unlike those who stutter, stammer, or, worst of all, forget. This is before the word "beautiful" exists in people's vocabulary, but "Oh, isn't she the *cutest* thing!" frequently floats my way. "And got so much sense!" they gratefully add...for which thoughtful addition I thank them to this day.

It was great fun being cute. But then, one day, it ended.

I am eight years old and a tomboy. I have a cowboy hat, cowboy boots, checkered shirt and pants, all red. My playmates are my brothers, two and four years older than I. Their colors are black and green, the only difference in the way we are dressed. On Saturday nights we all go to the picture show, even my mother: Westerns are her favorite kind of movie. Back home, "on the ranch," we pretend we are Tom Mix, Hopalong Cassidy, Lash LaRue (we've even named one of our dogs Lash LaRue); we chase each other for hours rustling cattle, being outlaws, delivering damsels from distress. Then my parents decide to buy my brothers guns. These are not "real" guns. They shoot "BBs," copper pellets my brothers say will kill birds. Because I am a girl, I do not get a gun. Instantly I am relegated to the position of Indian. Now there appears a great distance between us. They shoot and shoot at everything with their new guns. I try to keep up with my bow and arrows.

One day while I am standing on top of our makeshift "garage"—pieces of tin nailed across some poles—holding my bow and arrow and looking out toward the fields, I feel an incredible blow in my right eye. I look down just in time to see my brother lower his gun.

Both brothers rush to my side. My eye stings, and I cover it with my hand. "If you tell," they say, "we will get a whipping. You don't want that to happen, do you?" I do not. "Here is a piece of wire," says the older brother, picking it up from the roof; "say you stepped on one end of it and the other flew up and hit you." The pain is beginning to start. "Yes," I say. "Yes, I will say that is what happened." If I do not say this is what happened, I know my brothers will find ways to make me wish I had. But now I will say anything that gets me to my mother.

Confronted by our parents we stick to the lie agreed upon. They place me on a bench on the porch and I close my left eye while they examine the right. There is a tree growing from underneath the porch, that climbs past the railing to the roof. It is the last thing my right eye sees. I watch as its trunk, its branches, and then its leaves are blotted out by the rising blood.

I am in shock. First there is intense fever, which my father tries to break using lily leaves bound around my head. Then there are chills: my mother tries to get me to eat soup. Eventually, I do not know how, my parents learn what has happened. A week after the "accident" they take me to see a doctor. "Why did you wait so long to come?" he asks, looking into my eye and shaking his head. "Eyes are sympathetic," he says. "If one is blind, the other will likely become blind too."

This comment of the doctor's terrifies me. But it is really how I look that bothers me most. Where the BB pellet struck there is a glob of whitish scar tissue, a hideous cataract, on my eye. Now when I stare at people—a favorite pastime, up to now—they will stare back. Not at the "cute" little girl, but at her scar. For six years I do not stare at anyone because I do not raise my head.

Years later, in the throes of a mid-life crisis, I ask my mother and sister whether I changed after the "accident." "No," they say, puzzled. "What do you mean?"

What do I mean?

I am eight, and for the first time, doing poorly in school, where I have been something of a whiz since I was four. We have just moved to the place where the "accident" occurred. We do not know any of the people around us because this is a different county. The only time I see the friends I knew is when we go back to our old church. The new school is the former state penitentiary. It is a large stone building, cold and drafty, crammed to overflowing with boisterous, ill-disciplined children. On the third floor there is a huge circular imprint of some partition that has been torn out.

"What used to be there?" I ask a sullen girl next to me on our way past it to lunch.

"The electric chair," says she.

At night I have nightmares about the electric chair, and about all the people reputedly "fried" in it. I am afraid of the school, where all the students seem to be budding criminals.

"What's the matter with your eye?" they ask, critically.

When I don't answer (I cannot decide whether it was "accident" or not), they shove me, insist on a fight.

My brother, the one who created the story about the wire, comes to my rescue. But then brags so much about "protecting" me, I become sick.

After months of torture at the school, my parents decide to send me back to our old community to my old school. I live with my grandparents and the teacher they board. But there is not room for Phoebe, my cat. By the time my grandparents decide there is room, and I ask for my cat, she cannot be found. Miss Yarborough, the boarding teacher, takes me under her wing, and begins to teach me to play the piano. But soon she marries an African—a "prince," she says—and is whisked away to his continent.

At my old school there is at least one teacher who loves me. She is the teacher who "knew me before I was born" and bought my first baby clothes. It is she who makes my life bearable. It is her presence that finally helps me turn on the one child at the school who continually calls me "one-eyed bitch." One day I simply grab him by his coat and beat him until I am satisfied. It is my teacher who tells me my mother is ill.

My mother is lying in bed in the middle of the day, something I have never seen. She is in too much pain to speak. She has an abscess in her ear. I stand looking down on her, knowing that if she dies, I cannot live. She is being treated with warm oils and hot bricks held against her cheek. Finally a doctor comes. But I must go back to my grandparents' house. The weeks pass, but I am hardly aware of it. All I know is that my mother might die, my father is not so jolly, my brothers still have their guns, and I am the one sent away from home.

"You did not change," they say.

Did I imagine the anguish of never looking up?

I am twelve. When my relatives come to visit I hide in my room. My cousin Brenda, just my age, whose father works in the post office and whose mother is a nurse, comes to find me. "Hello," she says. And then she asks, looking at my recent school picture which I did not want taken, and on which the "glob" as I think of it is clearly visible, "You still can't see out of that eye?"

"No," I say, and flop back on the bed over my book.

That night, as I do almost every night, I abuse my eye. I rant and rave at it, in front of the mirror. I plead with it to clear up before morning. I tell it I hate and despise it. I do not pray for sight. I pray for beauty.

"You did not change," they say.

I am fourteen and baby-sitting for my brother Bill who lives in Boston. He is my favorite brother and there is a strong bond between us. Understanding my feelings of shame and ugliness, he and his wife take me to a local hospital where the "glob" is removed by a doctor named O. Henry. There is still a small bluish crater where the scar tissue was, but the ugly white stuff is gone. Almost immediately I become a different person from the girl who does not raise her head. Or so I think. Now that I've raised my head, I win the boyfriend of my dreams. Now that I've raised my head, I have plenty of friends. Now that I've raised my head, classwork comes from my lips as faultlessly as Easter speeches did, and I leave high school as valedictorian, most popular student and *queen*, hardly believing my luck. Ironically, the girl who was voted most beautiful in our class (and was) was later shot twice through the chest by a male companion, using a "real" gun, while she was pregnant. But that's another story in itself. Or, is it?

"You did not change," they say.

It is now thirty years since the "accident." A beautiful journalist comes to visit and to interview me. She is going to write a cover story for her magazine that focused on my last book. "Decide how you want to look on the cover," she says. "Glamorous, or whatever."

Never mind "glamorous," it is the "whatever" that I hear. Suddenly all I can think of is whether I will get enough sleep the night before the photography session: if I don't, my eye will be tired and wander, as blind eyes will.

At night in bed with my lover I think up reasons why I should not appear on the cover of the magazine. "My meanest critics will say I've sold out," I say. "My family will now realize I write scandalous books."

"But what's the real reason you don't want to do this?" he asks.

"Because in all probability," I say in a rush, "my eye won't be straight."

"It will be straight enough," he says. Then, "Besides, I thought you'd made your peace with that."

And I suddenly remember that I have.

I remember:

I am talking to my brother Jimmy, asking if he remembers anything unusual about the day I was shot. He does not know I consider that day the last time my father, with his sweet home remedy of cool lily leaves, "chose" me, and that I suffered and raged inside because of this. "Well," he says, "all I remember is standing by the side of highway with Daddy, trying to flag down a car. A white man stopped, but when Daddy said he needed somebody to take his little girl to the doctor, he drove off."

I remember:

I am in the desert for the first time. I fall totally in love with it. I am so overwhelmed by its beauty, I confront for the first time, consciously, the meaning of the doctor's words years ago: "Eyes are sympathetic. If one is blind, the other will likely become blind too." I realize I have dashed about the world madly, looking at this, looking at that, storing up images against the fading of the light. But I might have missed seeing the desert! The shock of that possibility—and gratitude for over twenty-five years of sight—sends me literally to my knees. Poem after poem comes—which is perhaps how poets pray.

On Sight

I am so thankful I have seen
The Desert
And the creatures in the desert
And the desert Itself.
The desert has it own moon
Which I have seen
With my own eye
There is no flag on it.
Trees of the desert have arms
All of which are always up
That is because the moon it up
The sun is up
Also the sky
The stars
Clouds
None with flags.
If there were flags, I doubt

the trees would point.
Would you?

But mostly, I remember this:

I am twenty-seven, and my baby daughter is almost three. Since her birth I have worried over her discovery that her mother's eyes are different from other people's. Will she be embarrassed? I wonder. What will she say? Every day she watches a television program called "Big Blue Marble." It begins with a picture of the earth as it appears from the moon. It is bluish, a little battered-looking, but full of light, with whitish clouds swirling around it. Every time I see it I weep with love, as if it is a picture of Grandma's house. One day when I am putting Rebecca down for her nap, she suddenly focuses on my eye. Something inside me cringes, gets ready to try to protect myself. All children are cruel about physical differences, I know from experience, and that they don't always mean to be is another matter. I assume Rebecca will be the same.

But no-o-o-o. She studies my face intently as we stand, her inside and me outside her crib. She even holds my face maternally between her dimpled little hands. Then, looking every bit as serious and lawyerlike as her father, she says, as if it may just possibly have slipped my attention: "Mommy, there a *world* in your eye." (As in, "Don't be alarmed, or do anything crazy.") And then, gently, but with great interest: "Mommy, where did you *get* that world in your eye?"

For the most part, the pain left then. (So what if my brothers grew up to buy even more powerful pellet guns for their sons and to carry real guns for themselves. So what if a young "Morehouse man" once nearly fell off the steps of Trevor Arnett Library because he thought my eyes were blue.) Crying and laughing I ran to the bathroom, while Rebecca mumbled and sang herself off to sleep. Yes indeed, I realized, looking in the mirror. There *was* a world in my eye. And I saw that it was possible to love it; that in fact, for all it had taught me, of shame and anger and inner vision, I *did* love it. Even to see it drifting out of orbit in boredom, or rolling up out of fatigue, not to mention floating back at attention in excitement (bearing witness, a friend has called it), deeply suitable to my personality, and even characteristic of me.

That night I dream I am dancing to Stevie Wonder's song "Always" (the name of the song is really "As," but I hear it as "Always.") As I dance, whirling and joyous, happier than I've ever been in my life, another bright-faced dancer joins me. We dance and kiss each other and hold each other through the night. The dancer has obviously come through all right, as I have done. She is beautiful, whole and free. And she is also me.

Below is a reflective response to Walker's essay.

When the Other Dancers Are, at First, My Sisters and Why I Don't Join Them Until Much Later

Andrea Devenney

I am very much unlike the child Alice Walker describes herself to be. I never could've presumed to be the prettiest, or expected to win a trip to the county fair because of my cuteness. I never would've performed an entire speech in front of an entire congregation without skipping a beat. I had a lisp, and I had to go to speech therapy twice each week to "cure" it. My sisters would've been like Alice Walker's brothers: playing active and imaginative games outside in the yard or in the basement. While Alice Walker's brothers relegated her to the position of Indian and she resented it, I relegated myself to the position of Indian to stay quiet. My sisters never would've shot me in the eye: but, as a too-early puberty-sodden ten-year-old, I shot myself a lot of times—and the wounds stayed there, in my eye, obscuring and damaging my self-image, until well after I stopped growing.

There's one picture where we are all supposed to be equally beautiful: it was taken on the front lawn before we left for our very last dance recital. My older sister Amy is wearing her tap costume: a red sequined leotard and a skirt of sheer white ruffles edged in the same scintillating scabs; my little sister Angela wears a ballet tutu of fine lavender net: her hair is hugged in place by a small silver tiara and many bobby pins; and I wear a fluorescent orange spandex jumpsuit with a neckline detail of gold fringe. Angela raises her arms above her head in a perfect circular arc, and Amy stands stylishly and confidently with her hands on her hips. They are both *smiling*. I am not. I am ten years old: already I am ill at ease with the proportions of my body—I am growing breasts, and spandex does not hide them; my armpits have sprouted a thin film of hair, and my dance costume is sleeveless.

The choreography for my dance routine, invented by the jazz teacher who looks like Nick Rhodes from Duran Duran, involves a lot of arm raising and jumping. This is meant to look energetic and electrifying: during class the dance teacher told us we ought to visualize ourselves as lightning bolts leaping down from the clouds. I cannot visualize myself as a lightning bolt because I am afraid of lightning. I want to ask the teacher if I can visualize myself as the rain puddle instead, but I am smart enough to know that puddles don't do much for the dynamics of dance routine creation. I want to tell the dance teacher I am absolutely certain that I will never become the lightning bolt. I am certain about this because lightning bolts do not have bee sting-sized boobies protruding from their chests, and it is also unlikely that they have moss-like hair growing under their armpits.

Like Alice Walker, I am painfully and consistently aware of how my scars change me, and change my life. Other people see my scars as plainly as I do, though I try to *minimize* the size of them by wearing my training bra on the tightest hook, and layering three shirts over that. I am very uncomfortable: I can hardly run and breathe at the same time during gym class, but I think binding my chest is a better option than squaring my shoulders and baring the scars' full weight. I know it is natural to have these scars, but I have trouble convincing myself of this. I do not want to be the only one saddled with two rapidly swelling scars. In the coatroom, a boy who always picks me to be on his kickball team tells me that I have big ones. He says this with a mixture of awe and sadness in his voice. I know now that I will not run as fast as I did before.

For two more years, I do not run as fast. The scars have continued swelling and all my shirts are abnormally snug across the chest. Alice Walker has to wait well into adulthood to reconcile with her scar, and it is her own daughter who helps initiate the peace. I do not have any peace until I start swimming class during the winter of eighth grade. In the locker room, I join the other girls in putting on the school-issue navy blue bathing suits. I notice that mine is the only suit that does not droop across the chest like a fabric frown. In class we practice the front crawl and the breaststroke. Other girls experience a rush of water down the front of their suits when they push off the pool wall and begin swimming. My bathing suit covers my chest like skin: it is flexible and accommodates my every move. I feel like a mermaid.

Alice Walker knows she is free from the burden of her scars when she dreams that she is dancing with another Alice Walker who is a beautiful and whole person. If my sisters and I took another picture wearing our dance costumes, I think that I would finally raise my arms above my head in a perfect arc—I shave now. I might even wear a tight shirt, because my scars are exactly the right size for my body proportions. And, undoubtedly, this time, I'd be smiling—as equally beautiful and whole as my sisters.

Exercise 7, Reflection Set 2

Teach Diversity—with a Smile

Barbara Ehrenreich

Something had to replace the threat of communism, and at last a workable substitute is at hand. "Multiculturalism" as the new menace is known, has been denounced in the media recently as the new McCarthyism, the new fundamentalism, even the new totalitarianism—take your choice. According to its critics, who include a flock of tenured conservative scholars, multiculturalism aims to toss out what it sees as the Eurocentric bias in education and replace Plato with Ntozake Shange and traditional math with the Yoruba number system. And that's just the beginning. The Jacobins of the multiculturalist movement, who are described derisively as P.C., or politically correct, are said to have launched a campus reign of terror against those who slip and innocently say "freshman" instead of "freshperson," "Indian" instead of "Native American" or, may the Goddess forgive them, "disabled" instead of "differently abled."

So you can see what is at stake here: freedom of speech, freedom of thought, Western civilization and a great many professional egos. But before we get carried away by the mounting backlash against multiculturalism, we ought to reflect for a moment on the system that the P.C. people aim to replace. I know all about it; in fact it's just about all I *do* know, since I—along with so many educated white people of my generation—was a victim of monoculturalism.

American history, as it was taught to us, began with Columbus's "discovery" of an apparently unnamed, unpeopled America, and moved on to the Pilgrims serving pumpkin pie to a handful of grateful red-skinned folks. College expanded our horizons with courses called Humanities or sometimes Civ, which introduced us to a line of thought that started with Homer, worked its way through Rabelais and reached a poignant climax in the pensées of Matthew Arnold. Graduate students wrote dissertations on what long-dead men had thought of Chaucer's verse or Shakespeare's dramas; foreign languages meant French or German. If there had been high technology in ancient China, kingdoms in Black Africa or women anywhere, at any time, doing anything worth noticing, we did not know it, nor did anyone think to tell us.

Our families and neighborhoods reinforced the dogma of monoculturalism. In our heads, most of us '50s teenagers carried around a social map that was about as useful as the chart that guided Columbus to the "Indies." There were "Negroes," "whites" and "Orientals," the latter meaning Chinese and "Japs." Of religions, only three were known—Protestant, Catholic and Jewish—and not much was known about the last two types. The only remaining human categories were husbands and wives, and that was all the diversity the monocultural world could handle. Gays, lesbians, Buddhists, Muslims, Malaysians, Mormons, etc. were simply off the map.

So I applaud—with one hand, anyway—the multiculturalist goal of preparing us all for a wider world. The other hand is tapping its fingers impatiently, because the critics are right about one thing: when advocates of multiculturalism adopt the haughty stance of political correctness, they quickly descend to silliness or worse. It's obnoxious, for example, to rely on university administrations to enforce P.C. standards of verbal inoffensiveness. Racist, sexist and homophobic thoughts cannot, alas, be abolished by fiat but only by the time-honored methods of persuasion, education and exposure to the other guy's—or, excuse me, woman's—point of view.

And it's silly to mistake verbal purification for genuine social reform. Even after all women are "Ms." and all people are "he or she," women will still earn only 65¢ for every dollar earned by men. Minorities by any other name, such as "people of color," will still bear a hugely disproportionate burden of poverty and discrimination. Disabilities are not just "different abilities" when there are not enough ramps for wheelchairs, signers for the deaf or special classes for the "specially" endowed. With all due respect for the new politesse, actions still speak louder than fashionable phrases.

But the worst thing about the P.C. people is that they are such poor advocates for the multicultural cause. No one was ever won over to a broader, more inclusive view of life by being bullied or relentlessly "corrected." Tell a 19-year-old white male that he can't say "girl" when he means "teen-age woman," and he will most likely snicker. This may be the reason why, despite the conservative alarms, P.C.-ness remains a relatively tiny trend. Most campuses have more serious and ancient problems: faculties still top-heavy with white males of the monocultural persuasion; fraternities that harass minorities and women; date rape; alcohol abuse, and tuition that excludes all but the upper fringe of the middle class.

So both sides would be well advised to lighten up. The conservatives ought to realize that criticism of the great books approach to learning do not amount to totalitarianism. And the advocates of multiculturalism need to regain the sense of humor that enabled their predecessors in the struggle to coin the term P.C. years ago—not in arrogance but in self-mockery.

Beyond that, both sides should realize that the beneficiaries of multiculturalism are not only the "oppressed peoples" on the standard P.C. list (minorities, gays, etc.). The "unenlightened"—the victims of monoculturalism—are oppressed too, or at least deprived.

Our educations, whether at Yale or at State U, were narrow and parochial and left us ill-equipped to navigate a society that truly is multicultural and is becoming more so every day. The culture that we studied was, in fact, *one* culture and, from a world perspective, all too limited and ingrown. Diversity is challenging, but those of us who have seen the alternative know it is also richer, livelier and ultimately more fun.

Below is a reflective response to Ehrenreich's essay.

Renouncing the Victims

Jonathan Edwards

For the most part, I agreed with Barbara Ehrenreich in her essay, "Teach Diversity—with a Smile." She's right that both sides of the "political correctness" debate need to step back and take a good, hard look at what they're really trying to accomplish. I further agree that most of these people could learn to "lighten up" just a little bit.

However, in some ways Ehrenreich is still thinking inside the box. Diversity training, even good, lighthearted diversity training is not the complete solution to a problem of closed dialogue, distrust, and disunity. In fact it's only a very small piece of the puzzle.

Diversity training was never part of my life growing up. I was taught at home from kindergarten through my senior year in high school. My background is conservative semi-fundamentalist Christian. I'm a middle-class, white male. Neither of my parents has ever been divorced. Almost all my friends before college were from church or home-school related activities. For the most part I led a very sheltered life.

I don't think that's entirely a bad thing though. I got to enjoy life as a kid, and I don't think I ended up unequipped to deal with a diverse and changing world. In her essay, Ehrenreich describes herself as a "victim of monoculturalism" (152). That's a funny way to phrase things. There are so many victims around. They're on TV, in the newspapers, walking around campus, in my classroom.

I could be a victim too. When I tell people I was home-schooled for twelve years, I usually get this very distinctive look. It's about half pity, mixed with a vague sort of fear—like I'm going to start shipping them letter bombs. The other half of the look registers surprise, and it's always followed by some variation of "Wow! You seem so normal."

The fact is, I could identify myself as a victim of my parent's choices and society's stereotypes. Very few of the home-schooled kids I know actually act like the socially repressed misfits people seem to think they should be. They are victims, but so are the people who stereotype them. We are all victims of something because we all are subjected to forces beyond our control. The farmer is victim of the drought. The driver is victim of the uninsured motorist. Barbara Ehrenreich is victim of monoculturalism. Her child may be victim of other kids toting deadly weapons to school.

Constant victimization cheapens the emotions we feel for the people who truly are victims. It disturbs me that when I see images like the destruction of the World Trade Center. I'm not nearly as shocked as I feel like I should be. Part of this is because I've seen buildings blowing up and people dying all the time in the movies and on television. Another aspect of this numbness, however, is I'm simply too used to feeling sorry for other people who are all victims of something.

People exist who truly are victims, but they can't all be that way. I can become a victim, but I cannot stay that way. The people we applaud are not the victims. They're the survivors, who brought something good out of tragedy or cruelty or background. As long as we remain victims, of monoculturalism or anything else, nothing will ever get done. We must move beyond victimization to achieve real change.

How do we make changes? Ehrenreich suggests we should "lighten up." *That* might not be a bad idea, but I want to suggest something even more basic—we need to listen. Listening should not be underrated. It's not a passive thing. It's very active, and it requires a lot of work. In his book *Civility,* Stephen Carter argues:

> If I expect you to listen respectfully to me and give me a genuine opportunity to convert you to my way of thinking, civility requires me to first listen respectfully to you and give you a genuine opportunity to convert me to your way of thinking. And there lies the risk…If I listen to you in a truly open way…I place my ego, my very sense of self, at hazard. In other words, instead of changing your mind, I might change mine. (139)

There is risk every time we try to communicate with others. We risk being rejected. We risk being misunderstood. We risk being fundamentally changed in ways we don't and can't anticipate (Edwards). Active listening changes us, and it changes our perspective of the world around us. It allows us to see people as people and not just victims of forces beyond their control.

I am not a victim of my background. I'm not sorry for it either. I'm grateful. It's part of what makes me unique. It's part of who I am. It's what I can bring to the table. That's what free speech and civil discourse is all about. Different perspectives must come together, and we must respect each other—not in a fluffy, politically correct way. True respect involves the strength of character to listen and the courage to disagree. Tolerance and political correctness are not enough when active listening and open dialogue is the goal.

I've learned to listen. I've learned to communicate. It's impossible for some kind of broad, sweeping, lesson plan change to teach students everything they need to know about everyone. When you teach about one group, you leave many others out, and there is only so much time in a day. Again, I'm not saying these changes are valueless, but they're a very small part that's been seriously overrated in everyone's mind. It's just not that simple. Many if not most of the well-educated people I've met have been poorly equipped to deal with someone like me. Don't teach people that we're all victims together. Teach them to listen, and the world opens up in ways society and the classroom simply cannot teach. I never had any diversity training—maybe that's just as well.

Works Cited

Carter, Stephen L. *Civility: Manners, Morals, and the Etiquette of Democracy.* New York: Basic Books, 1998.

Edwards, Jonathan J. "The Future of Rhetoric: Truth, Morality, and Civil Discourse." Unpublished paper, 2000.

Ehrenreich, Barbara. "Teach Diversity—with a Smile." *The Prentice Hall Guide to College Writers.* 5th ed. Ed. Stephen Reid. Upper Saddle River: Prentice Hall, 2000.

Exercise 9 Essay

Where's the Beef?

Alan Herscovici

With summer comes that most wonderful of North American traditions, the backyard barbeque. The succulent aroma of fresh grilled steak, sausages, chicken and fish draws family, friends and neighbours together for a communal feast. Inevitably, in these politically correct times, the conversation may drift to the question of whether we really ought to be eating meat at all.

The following guide should help you see through until the burgers are done.

Appealing to self-interest, a common opening line for proselytizing vegetarians is to claim that "eating meat is bad for us." They have trouble explaining, however, why human health and longevity have improved steadily as animal products became more readily available throughout this century. In fact, meat is an excellent source of 12 essential nutrients, including protein, iron, zinc and B vitamins.

It is true that excessive fats can be harmful, but today's meats are lean. Based on equal-size servings, tofu has more fat than a sirloin steak and only half the protein. (Tofu also makes a mess of the grill.)

With the exception of certain religious sects, people have rarely been vegetarian by choice. Most often, vegetarianism is the unfortunate result of poverty. Yet the veggie crowd also claims that "humans are not natural meat-eaters." Our teeth are not as sharp and our intestinal tracts not as short as those of cats and other pure carnivores. But we are not

"Where's the Beef" – From *Toronto Star*, May 27, 1998 by Alan Herscovici. Reprinted by permission.

95

equipped to be herbivores, either. Like other omnivores (such as bears or raccoons), our digestive equipment allows us to tackle a wide range of foods.

If we were not designed to eat meat, why do we produce large quantities of the enzymes required to break down such foods? Why is vitamin B12 (found only in animal products) essential to human life? If we were not natural meat-eaters, or at least bug and grub eaters, our species would have died out long ago. If we did not develop as hunters, why are our eyes in the front of our heads like those of other predators (tigers, wolves, or owls)? Why does the mere smell of a sizzling steak set my saliva glands watering?

Shifting their ground, animal activists now charge that livestock threatens the environment. But much of the world's arable land is best suited to be used as pasture. It is too hilly, fragile, dry or cold for cultivation. Cattle convert grass into nutrients that can be digested by humans. Those who promote organic agriculture understand that livestock completes the nutrient cycle by returning organic matter to the soil with manure.

Other anti-meat myths can also be dismissed. For example: Whatever you may think about fast food hamburgers, eating them does *not* encourage the destruction of the Amazon rainforests. Because of disease-control measures, no unprocessed South American beef products at all may be imported into Canada.

Livestock do *not* use up grains that could otherwise feed starving people in Third World countries. The main diet of cattle is grass and hay. Pigs, chickens, and other farm animals are generally fed corn and barley, while people eat mainly wheat and rice. Animals also consume pest- and weather-damaged grains, crop residues (corn stalks and leaves) and by-products from food processing, such as unusable grains (or parts of grains) left over from producing breakfast cereals and other human foods. Raising livestock in Canada does not prevent us from shipping emergency supplies to people in need. Hunger today, however, is usually the result of political, economic and distribution problems, not a lack of production capacity.

The production of methane gas by livestock is *not* a major contributor to global warming. Methane gas is only one of many possible "greenhouse" gases. It is produced by all sorts of decomposition of organic matter, including normal digestion (even by vegetarians). Main sources of greenhouse gases include wetlands, forest fires, landfills, rice paddies, the extraction of gas, oil and coal—and even termites.

Meat does *not* contain harmful pesticide, antibiotic or other residues. This is assured by stringent Agriculture Canada and Health Canada regulations and inspection. Concerns about dangerous bacteria are easily addressed by cooking your meat well. (Fruit and raw vegetables, in fact, present a more difficult problem.)

One study that is not often cited by animal activists is a recent report by the Centre for Energy and the Environment at the University of Exeter in England. David Coley and his associates analyzed how much fuel energy is used to produce and process different foods.

Burning fuel releases carbon into the atmosphere, the major suspected cause of global warning.

To the dismay of the politically correct set, meat scores far better than vegetables in this environmental-impact scale. It requires eight mega-joules of fuel energy to produce enough beef or burgers to provide one mega-joule of food energy. The fuel energy costs of chicken and lamb are seven mega-joules and six mega-joules respectively. Typical salad vegetables, however, require as much as 45 mega-joules of fuel energy for each energy unit of food intake provided.

"Meat does well because it is not highly processed, provides a lot of calories and is often produced locally," Coley reported in *New Scientist* last December.

It would require more ink than is available to us here to respond to all the claims animal activists have made about the supposed evils of modern livestock husbandry methods, what they misleadingly label "factory farming." For example, they criticize the caging of laying hens, while ignoring the fact that such systems improve hygiene, preventing disease and reducing the need for antibiotics.

Detailed responses to animal-welfare concerns are provided in *Food For Thought: Facts about Food and Farming,* published by the Ontario Farm Animal Council (7195 Millcreek Dr., Mississauga, Ont. L5N 4H1).

For debate around the barbeque, suffice it to say that animals cannot be productive unless they receive excellent nutrition and care. Farmers who do not provide good care for their animals will not remain in business for long.

Once fallacious claims about health, environment and animal welfare are stripped away, the heart of the animal-rights argument is exposed. What right, they ask, do we have to use animals at all?

The central fallacy of this argument is that it ignores basic principles of biology and ecology. Every plant and animal species naturally produces far more offspring than their environment can support to maturity. This "surplus" provides food for other species. Aboriginal people called this "the cycle of life." We now usually call it "the food chain." We are part of this cycle, like every other living organism on the planet. The domestication of livestock has been a very successful survival strategy, not only for humans, but also for the other species involved.

The squeamishness some people now feel about eating animals does not represent a more evolved sensitivity to nature. It is a symptom of how cut off some people have become from nature.

Thanks to modern agriculture, many city people now take our abundant food supply for granted. We forget that all our food must still be wrested from the land. Even our vegetables must be protected from other creatures. Even a carrot clings to the soil with all its strength. Like other animals, we kill to eat. But because we are human, we can also give thanks and treat the animals that feed us with respect.

I think those burgers should be ready about now.

Exercise 10 Essay

My 60-Second Protest from the Hallway

Emily Lesk

It's 8:32 A.M. School began two minutes ago. My bulging book bag is inside my first-period classroom saving my favorite seat. I am standing in the near-empty hallway, leaning against a locker right outside the classroom. I should be in class, yet my teacher has never objected to my minute-long absence, which has become a daily routine. I trace around the edges of the floor tiles with the toe of my running shoe, pausing several times to glance up at the second hand of the standard-issue clock mounted across the hall.

Although I have casually checked this clock countless times during my high-school career, this year looking at it has made me think about how significant 60 seconds can be. Last spring, the Commonwealth of Virginia passed a law that requires every public school in the state to set aside one minute at the beginning of each day during which students must remain seated while they "meditate, pray, or engage in any other silent activity." Every morning, at around 8:31, a resonant voice echoes over the school intercom. "Please rise for the Pledge of Allegiance." I stand up straight and salute the flag. After the pledge the voice commands me to "pause for a minute of silence." I push my chair under my desk and stride out of the classroom.

My objection to Virginia's Minute of Silence law is very simple. I see the policy as an attempt to bring organized prayer into the public schools, thus violating the United States Constitution. Last June at a statewide student-government convention, I spoke with state lawmakers, who confirmed my suspicion that the minute of silence is religiously motivated. One delegate proudly told me that she supported the law because reciting the Lord's Prayer had been a part of her own public-school education.

I agree with the law's strongest critics, who argue that it promotes religious discrimination because many faiths do not pray in the seated position mandated by the legislation. How would a Muslim third grader react to those students (and maybe a teacher) who might fold their hands and bow their heads to pray? Would she feel pressured to join in just to avoid criticism?

My opposition to this law is ironic because I consider myself religious and patriotic. I recite the Pledge of Allegiance daily (including the "one nation under God" part, which to me has historical, not religious, implications). As a Reform Jew, I get peace and self-assurance from religious worship and meditation, both at my synagogue and in my home. But my religious education also taught me the importance of standing up against discrimination and persecution.

In a school of 1,600 students, fewer than two dozen have joined me in protest. I usually walk out of class with one or two kids, sometimes none. Most days, when I glance back into the classroom, I see several students praying, heads bowed or eyes closed, while others do homework or daydream. Although I have not encountered any outright opposition, I often overhear classmates making sarcastic comments or dismissing the protest as futile. When I see that so many of my peers and teachers find no reason to question something I feel so strongly about, I wonder if my objection is justified. What do my 30 extra daily paces accomplish?

In contemplating that question, I've come to realize that taking a stand is about knowing why I believe what I do and refusing to give in despite the lack of support. My decision to protest was largely personal. Though I stayed in class the first morning the law was implemented—because I was caught off guard and because I was curious to see how others would respond—sitting there felt like a betrayal of my values. I also felt an obligation to act on behalf of the students all over Virginia who found their own beliefs violated but don't attend schools that allow them to express their opinions.

Deep down, I know this issue will be decided in a courtroom, not in my corridor. On May 8, the Fourth U.S. Circuit Court of Appeals heard oral arguments from ACLU lawyers representing seven families who are challenging the law, and will probably reach a decision over the summer. But for now I'll walk out of class each day to show my school community that an easy alternative to complacency does exist. This year I will have spent approximately three hours standing in the hallway in protest, watching the second hand make its 360-degree journey. As a senior about to graduate, I've thought a lot about the impact I've had on my school. I hope that my protest inspired other kids to use the time to think, not about a beckoning test, but about their views—even if those views differ from my own.

Sis! Boom! Bah! Humbug!

Rick Reilly

Every Friday night on America's high school football fields, it's the same old story. Broken bones. Senseless violence. Clashing egos.

Not the players. The cheerleaders.

According to a report by *The Physician and Sportsmedicine*, cheerleaders lose more time from their activity because of injury—28.8 days per injury—than any other group of athletes at the high school level. The University of North Carolina found that cheerleading is responsible for nearly half the high school and college injuries that lead to paralysis or death.

It's crazy, isn't it? We have girls building three-story human pyramids, flipping one another 30 feet in the air, and we give the *boys* helmets.

A buddy of mine has twin daughters, both cheerleaders. At the end of last school year one needed plastic surgery on her cheek after another girl's teeth went through it during a pyramid collapse; the other broke her hand and finger. They're not cheering anymore.

I don't hate cheerleading just because it's about as safe as porcupine juggling. I also hate it because it's dumb. The Velcroed-on smiles. The bizarre arm movements stolen from the Navy signalmen's handbook. The same cheers done by every troupe in every state.

What's even dumber is that cheerleaders have no more impact on the game than the night janitorial staff. They don't even face the game. They face the crowd, lost in their bizarre Muffy World. They cheer, they rah, they smile, they kiss, they hug. Meanwhile, Milford High just scored three touchdowns against their guys. A UFO could land at the 30-yard line, disgorging a chorus line of tiny, purple Ethel Mermans, and most cheerleaders would still be facing the other way yelling, "We got the fever!"

Exactly what does a girl get out of cheerleading, anyway, besides a circle skirt and a tight sweater? Why do we encourage girls to cheer the boys, to idolize the boys? Why do we want them on the sideline when most of them could be *between* the sidelines?

Studies show that by the time otherwise smart girls hit high school, they start to raise their hands less in class, let the boys take the lead. Isn't cheerleading the same thing, only outdoors?

Look, I married a cheerleader. My sisters were cheerleaders. I could see it then: Cheerleading was just about the only way a girl could be a part of sports. Not now. Not in the age of Mia Hamm and Marion Jones and the Williams sisters. Not when most high schools offer as many girls' sports as boys'.

Oh, right, nowadays cheerleading is classified as a sport. There are now "cheer gyms," where kids go to learn to throw each other around like Frisbees. You can even watch the National High School Cheerleading Championships on ESPN, just after the Harley-Davidson Olympics. This is the event in which 408 girls named Amber attempt to create a human Eiffel Tower, screaming, "Two! Four! Six! Eight!" while displaying all their gums at once. I'm not saying it isn't hard. I'm just saying it's pointless.

Do you realize colleges are even giving cheerleading scholarships? Can you believe that? *Sorry, Mrs. Roosevelt, we just gave away your daughter's chemistry scholarship. But you should have seen Amber here do "We've got spirit!"*

If cheerleading is a sport, Richard Simmons is a ballerina. It's athletic, but it's not a sport. In fact, what's sad is that most cheerleaders would make fine athletes. Watch for five minutes and you'll see. But these girls won't be on anybody's gymnastics or diving or basketball team because every season is cheerleading season.

Cheerleaders don't just shake their pom-poms at football games; they're also at baseball games and wrestling matches and girls' soccer games and most everything else short of chess-club tournaments. No matter how many hours they've already put in, no matter how freezing it is, no matter how few fans are at the jayvee badminton match, the cheerleaders are out there in the short skirts.

What's that spell? Frostbite?

If they're lucky, they might grow up to become Dallas Cowboys Cheerleaders. In the book *Deep in the Heart of Texas*, three former Cowboys Cheerleaders wrote that they snorted coke, gobbled diet pills and vomited to lose weight.

Rah!

I guess this is like coming out against fudge and kittens and Abe Lincoln, but it needs to be said. In four years my little girl hits high school. It's up to her, of course, but if my wife and I could choose her after-school activities, cheerleading would be next to last.

Just ahead of Piercing Club.

Below is a rhetorical analysis of Reilly's essay.

Like Asking Scrooge about Christmas

Mary Rosalez

According to the *American Internet Cheerleading Magazine,* there are more than three million high school and college cheerleaders in the United States, not to mention the millions in Japan, Europe, Australia, Canada, and Mexico. Cheerleading began at Princeton University in 1898 with a man named Johnny Campbell, a fan who couldn't control his enthusiasm at a football game and got out in front of the crowd and started yelling. From there it has grown into a competitive sport for both men and women involving dance, gymnastics, and teamwork. Yet not everyone likes cheerleading or thinks of it as a sport. One such person is Rick Reilly, a columnist for *Sports Illustrated.* In an effort to depict cheerleading as the most frivolous and senseless of activities for young girls, Reilly's editorial "Sis! Boom! Bah! Humbug!" from the May 2000 issue of *Sports Illustrated* runs down cheerleaders and cheerleading with a semi full of sarcasm. He claims to have "married a cheerleader" and that his "sisters were cheerleaders" (9), but that at the time they had no other athletic opportunities. Girls today, he says, should be *between* the sidelines," (7, emphasis his) not on them. Cheerleading, he says, is "dumb" (5). While some of Reilly's points are compelling, his overwhelming sarcastic tone damages both his ethos and his logos, resulting in an unsuccessful editorial that makes even a cheerleading skeptic defensive of the sport.

If one is trying to find fault with cheerleading, Reilly's use of statistics about the dangers of cheerleading, along with the graphic anecdote of his friend's injured twin cheerleaders, makes sense. He begins his article by talking about the "same old story. Broken bones. Senseless violence. Clashing egos" (1). He is not talking about football players but cheerleaders. And it is true; cheerleading can be dangerous. I have personally seen some pretty gruesome tumbles. His logos, then, begins strong. Just stating the fact that "cheerleading is responsible for nearly half the high school and college injuries that lead to paralysis or death" (2) gets readers listening right away. Too, Reilly's source, the University of North Carolina, is credible. I am convinced that cheerleading is indeed dangerous by this single statistic. But Reilly does not stay on this vein of logic for long.

Reilly fumbles when, in only the fifth paragraph, he falls to mockery; there is no logic in saying that cheerleading is "dumb." He resorts to stereotyping, depicting cheerleaders as bimbo blondes with "Velcroed-on smiles" that have "no more impact on the game than the night janitorial staff" (6). How does he know that the smiles of these girls are insincere? Does he ever show evidence that they have no impact on the game? Are there any surveys? Did he talk to anyone at a game and ask them? He does none of these things. He simply says them and we're supposed to agree. I want to ask him how he knows such things, even if I may believe them to be true. Who does he think he is to be so cruel? The sarcasm, then, rather than making readers laugh and nod, makes us defensive of these girls.

In another seeming attempt at logic, Reilly compares the value of a cheerleading scholarship to a chemistry scholarship; however, this is a different argument altogether, the awarding of sports vs. academic scholarships. Why doesn't he compare it to a football scholarship? He doesn't because he knows that many people are outraged at college football scholarships, not because football players are stereotypically dumb or because Mrs. Smith doesn't see the value in football, but because it gives students money to get an education for playing a sport; many people don't believe the two should mix. But Reilly doesn't compare a cheerleading scholarship even to football. No, to chemistry. And when he imagines the outcry of parents at this horrendous development, his sarcasm crosses the line: "*Sorry, Mrs. Roosevelt,* [notice the name-dropping!] *We just gave away your daughter's chemistry scholarship. But you should have seen Amber here do 'We've got spirit!'*" (11, emphasis his). At first glance this may seem logical, to compare the two scholarships, but there is no logic. This does *not* happen. Students don't lose chemistry scholarships to cheerleaders. Besides, the argument is off-topic, has nothing really to do with cheering being dangerous or a blow to feminism or even stupid; instead, it makes Reilly seem "dumb."

Because Reilly does not rely heavily on logos, the effect is one of assumption: Reilly assumes his readers have been to sporting events, seen these stereotypically blonde bimbos, heard their mindless hoorahs, and witnessed their lack of effectiveness with the spectators. Although at first this assumption seems valid considering his audience—*Sports Illustrated* readers—the fact is that he isn't just assuming his readers have witnessed cheerleading, but that they, too, do not think it important. This is a dangerous assumption, to think you know the preferences of such a wide audience. There is no logic to stereotyping; it's narrow-minded and chauvinistic. The result is an editorial that, while it contains a modicum of logic, does not hold enough to overpower the stench of his offensive sarcasm.

Emotionally, Reilly's sarcasm tends to lighten his article and lend humor to his subject. While a reader may feel disgusted at the thought of a "girl's teeth [going] through [another's cheek] during a pyramid collapse" (4) or appalled at the three Dallas cheerleaders who "snorted coke, gobbled diet pills and vomited to lose weight" (14), the rest of Reilly's images and language are intended to be funny. Someone like my father, who has always hated cheerleading, would think Reilly hilarious. My dad makes similar comments every time he watches football. But the general audience is not going to consist of 80-year-old retired engineers. When this kind of sarcasm is poured on so heavily to an audience that may or may not agree that cheerleading is goofy fluff, the response is to believe that Reilly never considered the scope of his audience. Reilly never considers those who may love cheering—or even those who have never thought about it much. After listening to years of my dad's remarks, I tend to think of cheerleading as less than integral to a game. But my reaction to this article was emotional: I suddenly wanted to defend cheerleading as a valid sport and cheerleaders as talented and dedicated young women.

Reilly never comes right out and says cheerleading should be done away with; he just says it's "pointless" (10). He never *says* cheerleaders are dumb; he just says that "a UFO could land at the 30-yard line [...] and most cheerleaders would still be facing the other way yelling, 'We got the fever!'" (6). He never says cheerleading is *not* a sport; he just says, "Oh, right, nowadays cheerleading is classified as a sport" (10). It's those first few words—"Oh, right [...]"—that let us know he thinks it's dumb to consider it one. His gross over-generalization of the cheerleader type—speaking in a way that borders on bigotry—just makes me mad. How can he say, even with tongue-in-cheek, that the National High School Cheerleading Championships "is the event in which 408 girls named Amber attempt to create a human Eiffel Tower, screaming, 'Two! Four! Six! Eight!' while displaying all their gums at once" (10). I've watched this event; it's nothing of the sort.

Reilly stereotypes cheerleaders as nothing more than marshmallow fluff on the red velvet cake of every game by asking questions like: "Exactly what does a girl get out of cheerleading, anyway, besides a circle skirt and a tight sweater?" (7). He doesn't bother to answer. As a result, *we* want to answer this rhetorical question; we want to tell him that cheerleading promotes the same ideals as any sport. He does admit that "nowadays cheerleading is classified as a sport" (10). But does Reilly bother to define "sport" in any way? No. He never talks about why any sport is valued, why we consider bouncing a pumpkin-like ball back and forth and tossing it in a hoop is valuable, why going back and forth in a pool fastest is valuable, why jumping over a high bar is valuable. He never talks of the benefits of camaraderie and teamwork, of dedication and exercise that are considered the benefits of every sport and are certainly present in the sport of cheerleading. He simply continues on with the sarcasm, saying that "if cheerleading is a sport, Richard Simmons is a ballerina" (12), making fun of girls who have been made fun of for years. It's old. Instead of being funny, he simply sounds grouchy and opinionated. His sarcasm, poured on so heavily, is no longer funny. It's like eating a whole cake alone: there comes a point where what could be wonderful becomes nauseating. His attempt at humor as pathos fails.

Reilly does make a small stab at a moral approach to cheerleading—or rather anti-cheerleading: he would like to see girls taking the lead from the boys, rather than idolizing them as he assumes cheerleaders do. But he doesn't take this argument very far. He never discusses how cheerleading does, in fact, put girls below or behind boys. He does bring up unidentified "studies" (8) which claim that "by the time otherwise smart girls hit high school, they start to raise their hands less in class, let the boys take the lead. Isn't cheerleading the same thing, only outdoors?" (8). But the connection is weak; we don't know what the "surveys" were for—whether psychological, pedagogical, or medical—and the idea is taken out of context. This argument begs the question: *are* boys taking the lead when girls cheer? Perhaps he is saying that cheerleaders are falling into a patriarchal role where boys do the work and girls provide moral support. But this idea falls right through the cracks when we remember that there are a significant number of male cheerleaders, some of whom ended up to be quite famous. Kirk Douglas was a cheerleader. Ronald Reagan, Franklin D. Roosevelt and George W. Bush were cheerleaders. Even John Wayne was a cheerleader! It's difficult to imagine these men as idolizers of football players, as sissies and followers rather than leaders, as "girls named Amber" who "shake their pom-poms [sic]" (13). Reilly didn't bother to find out that 83% of cheerleaders carry a B average or above in their courses, 62% are involved in a second sport, and 83% are leaders in student organizations. These young ladies—and men—are not all dopey puppies following around the big, tough football players with their tongues hanging out.

Reilly's idea of cheering as idolizing breaks down even more when he says the girls "don't even face the game" (5). How does it stand to reason, then, that these girls are followers of boys, living in their shadow, if they don't really pay attention, if "They cheer, they rah, they smile, they kiss, they hug. Meanwhile, Milford High [scores] three touchdowns against their guys" (6)? His attempt at sounding like he actually cares about these girls—assuming they are all girls, of course—and their roles in a patriarchal society falls flat, especially since Reilly has already established himself as a grouch who doesn't think much of cheerleaders. If he wants to act like he cares, he shouldn't call them dumb.

Halfway through the article, Reilly takes a stab at redeeming his credibility by saying that his wife and sisters were cheerleaders (9). It seems that he is trying to establish that he is not prejudiced against cheerleaders—that maybe this makes him sympathetic or knowledgeable—that he couldn't possibly despise the past choices of his own family, and he certainly would never call his wife dumb. But it's too late. We already know Reilly is a Scrooge, that he has as much compassion for cheerleaders as Ebenezer did for poor old Cratchitt. Who would listen to Scrooge's evaluation of Christmas? Only those who already hated the season, too. Obviously someone so jaded is not a reliable source. When I read this, it occurred to me that my mom, too, was a cheerleader. She has been married to my dad for 55 years. Apparently this does not prevent my dad—or Reilly—from "hat[ing] cheerleading because it's dumb" (5). As a grouchy, opinionated man who doesn't seem genuinely concerned about the girls who cheer, his ethos flounders and falls flat on its face. Too much sarcasm, it seems, can be more dangerous than a tower of cheering girls.

Reilly, at the last second, admits that he may be offending someone: "I guess this is like coming out against fudge and kittens and Abe Lincoln, but it needs to be said" (15). Unfortunately, even this tiny poke at self-redemption fails. This is not an argument; it's *ad populum.* Those who support cheerleading don't do so because it's yummy or cuddly or All-American; they believe in its value because they believe in sportsmanship and moral support. They consider themselves athletes even if Reilly and my dad don't. At this point,

Reilly's attempt at logic is ridiculous, his pathos of sarcasm has turned to bigotry, and as a result he has lost all respect and authority.

Reilly's article has little redeeming value as a rhetorically convincing piece. His ethos is untrustworthy, narrow-minded—or at least playfully prejudiced—and slanted. Because he never makes an effort to talk to an actual cheerleader or fan, because his attempt to sound caring is overwhelmed by ridicule, he is not to be considered credible. His pathos relies completely—and fatally—on sarcasm; the heavy load of Reilly's cynicism hardly convinces a reader of anything but a bad attitude on the writer's part. Reilly's logos is so muddled and without convincing evidence that it becomes locos. What few logical points he has are swallowed in the pathos of ridicule. While Reilly's article may appeal to my father, it does not carry with it the weight of authority, the pull of emotion, nor the appeal to reason that would sway any sensible reader to thinking cheerleading is as dumb as he would like to make it. I'm envisioning Reilly watching the National Cheerleading Championships with my dad; it would be like Scrooge and Marley sitting in church on Christmas Day. [2,384 words]

Exercise 13, Rhetorical Analysis Set 2

Sticks and Stones and Sports Team Names

Richard Estrada

When I was a kid living in Baltimore in the late 1950s, there was only one professional sports team worth following. Anyone who ever saw the movie *Diner* knows which one it was. Back when we liked Ike, the Colts were the gods of the grid-iron and Memorial Stadium was their Mount Olympus.

Ah, yes: The Colts, The Lions, Da Bears. Back when defensive tackle Big Daddy Lipscomb was letting running backs know exactly what time it was, a young fan could easily forget that in a game where men were men, the teams they played on were not invariably named after animals. Among others, the Packers, the Steelers, and the distant 49ers were cases in point. But in the roll call of pro teams, one name in particular always discomfited me: The Washington Redskins. Still, however willing I may have been to go along with the name as a kid, as an adult I have concluded that using an ethnic group essentially as a sports

"Team Names Demonstrate Intensity" – From *Dallas Morning News*, October 27, 1995 by Richard Estrada. Copyright © 1995 by Dallas Morning News. Reprinted by permission.

mascot is wrong.

By no means were such names originally meant to disparage Native Americans. The noble symbols of the Redskins or college football's Florida Seminoles or the Illinois Illini are meant to be strong and proud. Yet, ultimately, the practice of using a people as mascots is dehumanizing. It sets them apart from the rest of society. It promotes the politics of racial aggrievement at a moment when our storehouse is running over with it.

The World Series between the Cleveland Indians and the Atlanta Braves reignited the debate. In the chill night air of October, tomahawk chops and war chants suddenly became far more familiar to millions of fans, along with the ridiculous and offensive cartoon logo of Cleveland's "Chief Wahoo."

The defenders of team names that use variations on the Indian theme argue that tradition should not be sacrificed at the altar of political correctness. In truth, the nation's No. 1 P.C. [politically correct] school, Stanford University, helped matters some when it changed its team nickname from "the Indians" to "the Cardinals [sic]." To be sure, Stanford did the right thing, but the school's status as P.C. without peer tainted the decision for those who still need to do the right thing.

Another argument is that ethnic group leaders are too inclined to cry wolf in alleging racial insensitivity. Often, this is the case. But no one should overlook genuine cases of political insensitivity in an attempt to avoid accusations of hypersensitivity and political correctness.

The real world is different from the world of sports entertainment. I recently heard a father who happened to be a Native American complain on the radio that his child was being pressured into participating in celebrations of Braves baseball. At his kid's school, certain days are set aside on which all children are told to dress in Indian garb and celebrate with tomahawk chops and the like.

That father should be forgiven for not wanting his family to serve as somebody's mascot. The desire to avoid ridicule is legitimate and understandable. Nobody likes to be trivialized or deprived of their dignity. This has nothing to do with political correctness and the provocations of militant leaders.

Against this backdrop, the decision by newspapers in Minneapolis, Seattle and Portland to ban references to Native American nicknames is more reasonable than some might think.

What makes naming teams after ethnic groups, particularly minorities, reprehensible is that politically important groups continue to be targeted, while politically powerful ones who bit back are left alone. How long does anyone think the name "Washington Blackskins" would last? Or how about "the New York Jews?"

With no fewer than 10 Latino ballplayers on the Cleveland Indians' roster, the team could change its name to "the Banditos." The trouble is, they would be missing the point:

Latinos would correctly object to that stereotype, just as they rightly protested against Frito-Lay's use of the "Frito Bandito" character years ago.

It seems to me that what Native Americans are saying is that what would be intolerable for Jews, blacks, Latinos and others is no less offensive to them. Theirs is a request not only for dignified treatment, but for fair treatment as well. For America to ignore the complaints of a numerically small segment of the population because it is small is neither dignified nor fair.

Below is a rhetorical analysis of Estrada's essay

The Right Idea, the Wrong Argument

Angie Fenton Freidman

Using Native American Indians as the nomenclature for sports team names is wrong for a number of reasons. Yet, Richard Estrada, in his essay "Sticks and Stones and Sports Team Names," does not argue this claim effectively. Estrada, utilizing ethos and pathos appeals, fails in his use of the rhetorical appeals of authority, assertion, analogy, and allusion. Instead, he chooses to devise an approach that provokes anger and confusion at his choice of strategy, rather than evoking persuasion or agreement from his argument. Using natives to name sports teams is wrong, but Estrada doesn't prove this with his editorial.

"For America to ignore the complaints of a numerically small segment of the population because it is small is neither dignified nor fair," Estrada states, but in doing so he diminishes the real argument: sports teams have not used other segments of the population to name themselves because it is easier to degrade Native Americans than any other ethnic group simply because everybody does it. Estrada purposely uses the words "fair" and "dignified" to argue his assertion, but these terms are so weak and commonplace that they do not carry the weight needed in such an argument, and they compel those who detest the usage of natives in the naming of teams to feel anger toward Estrada's almost light-hearted assertion. Using natives to name sports teams is degrading, blatantly offensive, and positively disgusting. Fairness and dignity take second place in the debate.

In one reference, Estrada chooses to compare calling the Washington Redskins the "Washington Blackskins" or the New York Giants the "New York Jews." These are certainly stronger comparisons than the Washington White Guys, which many white people have found humor in, but he could have chosen to use even stronger analogies, such as the "Hawaii Homosexuals," the "Cincinnati Spics" or the "Baltimore Bitches." Using "Blackskins" as an example was effective, but not effective enough. Blacks are the minority population deemed most likely to be accepted in society in part because of their numbers. Although Hispanics outnumber blacks, black people have been a major part of the United States' history longer and have, therefore, been a part of the acceptance process longer. Using blacks and Jews as analogies was not a word choice that carries as much weight as the aforementioned terms—terms that target segments of the population who are continually disrespected and belittled. Estrada fails to ignite emotion in his readers—though he tries—when using these terms. We know "Blackskins" and "Jews" would not be used because they simply would not be used. But, sadly, Native Americans do not own that same respect (nor do Hispanics, homosexuals, and, sometimes, women) and in his essay, Estrada makes this point clear—the possession of respect by one group and the failure to obtain that same respect by another—through his use of selected analogies, though that does not seem to be what he purported to do in the first place. By trying to argue one claim but ending up arguing another, Estrada continues to lose steam and confuse his audience.

Estrada states, "By no means were such names originally meant to disparage Native Americans." In an attempt to exhibit authority, and Estrada clearly believes this statement to be true, the author not only misleads his audience, but he contradicts himself two sentences later by asserting, "Yet, ultimately, the practice of using a people as mascots is dehumanizing." Either such a practice is disparaging and dehumanizing or it isn't, but Estrada wants it both ways. Perhaps the most damaging use of this appeal is that it is simply not true. According to Todd Williamson, assistant director of Native American Programs at CMU, the Cleveland Indians named their team as such to honor the native baseball players on their team. Williamson said, however, that very few Native Americans have been consulted in the naming of other sports teams, and that no one ever consulted any natives in the naming of the Washington Redskins. What Estrada states as fact, with authority, is simply not true. The naming of sports teams was indeed meant to be disparaging and dehumanizing. The intimidating symbolism associated with the "noble savage scalping the settlers," Williamson said, cannot be comprehended as anything but disparaging, especially in an era in which Native Americans are as productive a people as any other segment of the population.

Estrada uses the appeal of allusion when he refers to the current number of Latino members on the Cleveland Indians team. "...[T]he team could change its name to 'the Banditos,'" Estrada writes. Except that the Hispanic equivalent of "Indians" is not "Banditos." Banditos is the Latino word for "robber" or "bandit." If Estrada had alluded to the use of "Redskins" in correlation with "Banditos" (two disparaging terms used to stereotype and dehumanize the people they refer to), then this allusion would have worked. Once again, Estrada is off the mark and his use of allusion falls flat.

Estrada's inclusion of the childhood chant "Sticks and stones..." is ironic. We know that words can often hurt much more than physical injury and Estrada's editorial—his use of language—hurts the debate of using natives for naming sports teams. His words are confusing, his analogies weak, his authority simply wrong, and his allusions off base. In an attempt at establishing ethos, Estrada ruins his credibility by not checking his facts. And the pathos appeal only results in angering those who agree that the sports team names are wrong because Estrada has done nothing to further that cause, justifying the decision to name teams as such for those who believe there isn't any validity in the debate and that names are just that, and confusing everyone, regardless of where one stands in the debate. [958 words]

Exercise 17, Essays about Poverty in America

What is Poverty?

Jo Goodwin Parker

You ask me what is poverty? Listen to me. Here I am, dirty, smelly, and with no "proper" underwear on and with the stench of my rotting teeth near you. I will tell you. Listen to me. Listen without pity. I cannot use your pity. Listen with understanding. Put yourself in dirty, worn out, ill-fitting shoes, and hear me.

Poverty is getting up every morning from a dirt- and illness-stained mattress. The sheets have long since been used for diapers. Poverty is living in a smell that never leaves. This is a smell of urine, sour milk, and spoiling food sometimes joined with the strong smell of long-cooked onions. Onions are cheap. If you have smelled this smell, you did not know how it came. It is the smell of the outdoor privy. It is the smell of young children who cannot walk the long dark way at night. It is the smell of the mattresses where years of "accidents" have happened. It is the smell of the milk which has gone sour because the refrigerator long has not worked, and it costs money to get it fixed. It is the smell of rotting garbage. I could bury it, but where is the shovel? Shovels cost money.

Poverty is being tired. I have always been tired. They told me at the hospital when the last baby came that I had chronic anemia caused from poor diet, a bad case of worms, and that I needed a corrective operation. I listened politely—the poor are always polite. The poor always listen. They don't say that there is no money for iron pills, or better food, or worm medicine. The idea of an operation is frightening and costs so much that, if I had dared, I would have laughed. Who takes care of my children? Recovery from an operation takes a long time. I have three children. When I left them with "Granny" the last time I had a job, I came home to find the baby covered with fly specks, and a diaper that had not been changed since I left. When the dried diaper came off, bits of my baby's flesh came with it. My other child was playing with a sharp bit of broken glass, and my oldest was playing alone at the edge of a lake. I made twenty-two dollars a week, and a good nursery school costs twenty dollars a week for three children. I quit my job.

Poverty is dirt. You can say in your clean clothes coming from your clean house, "Anybody can be clean." Let me explain about housekeeping with no money. For breakfast I give my children grits with no oleo or cornbread without eggs and oleo. This does not use up many dishes. What dishes there are, I wash in cold water and with no soap. Even the cheapest soap has to be saved for the baby's diapers. Look at my hands, so cracked and red. Once I saved for two months to buy a jar of Vaseline for my hands and the baby's diaper rash. When I had saved enough, I went to buy it and the price had gone up two cents. The baby and I suffered on. I have to decide everyday if I can bear to put my cracked sore hands into the cold water and strong soap. But you ask, why not hot water? Fuel costs money. If you have a wood fire it costs money. If you burn electricity, it costs money. Hot water is a luxury. I do not have luxuries. I know you will be surprised when I tell you how young I am. I look so much older. My back has been bent over the wash tubs every day for so long, I cannot remember when I ever did anything else. Every night I wash every stitch my school age child has on and just hope her clothes will be dry by morning.

Poverty is staying up all night on cold nights to watch the fire knowing one spark on the newspaper covering the walls means your sleeping child dies in flames. In summer poverty is watching gnats and flies devour your baby's tears when he cries. The screens are torn and you pay so little rent you know they will never be fixed. Poverty is hoping it never rains because diapers won't dry when it rains and soon you are using newspapers. Poverty is seeing your children forever with runny noses. Paper handkerchiefs cost money and all your rags you need for other things. Even more costly are antihistamines. Poverty is cooking without food and cleaning without soap.

Poverty is asking for help. Have you ever had to ask for help, knowing your children will suffer unless you get it? Think about asking for a loan from a relative, if this is the only way you can imagine asking for help. I will tell you how it feels. You find out where the office is that you are supposed to visit. You circle that block four or five times. Thinking of your children, you go in. Everyone is very busy. Finally, someone comes out and you tell her you need help. That never is the person you need to see. You go see another person, and after spilling the whole shame of your poverty all over the desk between you, you find that this isn't the right office after all—you must repeat the whole process, and it never is any easier at the next place.

You have asked for help, and after all it has a cost. You are again told to wait. You are told why, but you don't really hear because of the red cloud of shame and the rising cloud of despair.

Poverty is remembering. It is remembering quitting school in junior high because "nice" children had been so cruel about my clothes and my smell. The attendance officer came. My mother told him I was pregnant. I wasn't, but she thought that I could get a job and help out. I had jobs off and on, but never long enough to learn anything. Mostly I remember being married. I was so young then. I am still young. For a time, we had all the things you have. There was a little house in another town, with hot water and everything. Then my husband lost his job. There was unemployment insurance for a while and what few jobs I could get. Soon, all our nice things were repossessed and we moved back here. I was pregnant then. This house didn't look so bad when we first moved in. Every week it gets worse. Nothing is ever fixed. We now had no money. There were a few odd jobs for my husband, but everything went for food then, as it does now. I don't know how we lived through three years and three babies, but we did. I'll tell you something, after the last baby I destroyed my marriage. It had been a good one, but could you keep on bringing children in this dirt? Did you ever think how much it costs for any kind of birth control? I knew my husband was leaving the day he left, but there were no goodbyes between us. I hope he has been able to climb out of this mess somewhere. He never could hope with us to drag him down.

That's when I asked for help. When I got it, you know how much it was? It was, and is, seventy-eight dollars a month for the four of us; that is all I ever can get. Now you know why there is no soap, no needles and thread, no hot water, no aspirin, no worm medicine, no hand cream, no shampoo. None of these things forever and ever and ever. So that you can see clearly, I pay twenty dollars a month rent, and most of the rest goes for food. For grits and cornmeal, and rice and milk and beans. I try my best to use only the minimum electricity. If I use more, there is that much less for food.

Poverty is looking into a black future. Your children won't play with my boys. They will turn to other boys who steal to get what they want. I can already see them behind bars of their prison instead of behind the bars of my poverty. Or they will turn to the freedom of alcohol or drugs, and find themselves enslaved. And my daughter? At best, there is for her a life like mine.

But you say to me, there are schools. Yes, there are schools. My children have no extra books, no magazines, no extra pencils, or crayons, or paper and most important of all, they do not have health. They have worms, they have infections, they have pink-eye all summer. They do not sleep well on the floor, or with me in my one bed. They do not suffer from hunger, my seventy-eight dollars keeps us alive, but they do suffer from malnutrition. Oh yes, I do remember what I was taught about health in school. It doesn't do much good. In some places there is a surplus commodities program. Not here. The country said it cost too much. There is a school lunch program. But I have two children who will already be damaged by the time they get to school.

But, you say to me, there are health clinics. Yes, there are health clinics and they are in the towns. I live out here eight miles from town. I can walk that far (even if it is sixteen miles both ways), but can my children? My neighbor will take me when he goes; but he expects to get paid, *one way or another.* I bet you know my neighbor. He is that large man who spends his time at the gas station, the barbershop, and the corner store complaining about the government spending money on the immoral mothers of illegitimate children.

Poverty is an acid that drips on pride until all pride is worn away. Poverty is a chisel that chips on honor until honor is worn away. Some of you say that you would do *something* in my situation, and maybe you would, for the first week or the first month, but for year after year after year?

Even the poor can dream. A dream of a time when there is money. Money for the right kinds of food, for worm medicine, for iron pills, for toothbrushes, for hand cream, for a hammer and nails and a bit of screening, for a shovel, for a bit of paint, for some sheeting, for needles and thread. Money to pay *in money* for a trip to town. And, oh, money for hot water and money for soap. A dream of when asking for help does not eat away the last bit of pride. When the office you visit is as nice as the offices of other governmental agencies, where there are enough workers to help you quickly, when workers do not quit in defeat and despair. When you have to tell your story to only one person, and that person can send you for other help and you don't have to prove your poverty over and over and over again.

I have come out of my despair to tell you this. Remember I did not come from another place or another time. Others like me are all around you. Look at us with an angry heart, anger that will help you help me. Anger that will let you tell of me. The poor are always silent. Can you be silent too?

After Katrina, Pleas for a Focus on Poverty

John Dart

After Hurricane Katrina produced vivid images of poverty in America, leaders of five mainline denominations renewed their call on Congress to oppose deep cuts to programs serving the working poor, children, and seniors.

On the day that New Orleans flooded, the Census Bureau said that the number of Americans living in poverty had risen for the fourth straight year. "Our denominations have mobilized and are responding in prayer and financial support and direct service to those in need," the leaders wrote. "Yet, just as disaster struck the Gulf Coast, the U.S. Census Bureau reported in very particular detail that poverty in the United States is growing."

The plea in mid-September by Episcopal, Methodist, Presbyterian, Lutheran, and

United Church of Christ officials coincided with broader political pleas for serious attempts in Washington to prepare for future disasters—both natural and human-produced—that take the heaviest toll on people with few or no fallback resources.

"September 11 made Americans aware of our national security vulnerability," said Andrew Kohut, president of the Pew Research Center, as quoted by the *Los Angeles Times,* "and there is a good chance that Katrina will raise the public's consciousness about the weakness of our social safety net."

John Edwards, the 2004 Democratic vice presidential nominee, said in a CNN program, "One of the things that I hope we will do is look at this as an opportunity . . . to shine a bright light on poverty in America and do something about it nationally."

And on ABC's *This Week* Senator Barack Obama (D., Ill.) said the crisis should move the two parties to overcome "the false dichotomy" over whether the key to reducing poverty is more government help (Democrats) or greater responsibility among the poor (Republicans). Both are required, Obama said.

If awareness of the sharp political divisions in the nation's capital were not enough to invite some cynical shrugs regarding such hopes, the United Nations summit against poverty a few days later elicited skepticism because of the way it has been overshadowed by the UN's oil-for-food scandal and disagreements over proposed reforms of the international body.

Religious leaders who met earlier at the Washington National Cathedral are urging national leaders from around the world to live up to their responsibility and cut the rate of extreme global poverty by 2015, an aim of the Millennium Development Goals agreed to by the UN in 2000. They also seek a partnership between governments and religious institutions on development problems.

At the cathedral, former U.S. secretary of state Madeline Albright and others decried on September 11 suggestions by John R. Bolton, the U.S. ambassador to the UN, that the United States wants to downplay the importance of the Millennium goals. As reported by the *New York Times,* Bolton initially proposed—though he subsequently relented—deleting any reference to specific goals for reducing poverty, hunger and child mortality and combating such pandemics as AIDS, preferring instead to cite broadly stated goals.

Some 30 Christian leaders from Anglican, Protestant, Roman Catholic, Orthodox and other traditions issued a statement prior to the UN gathering that said, among other things, "The increasing concentration of wealth in our world, while so many suffer, is a scandal to us all."

Ishmael Noko, general secretary of the Lutheran World Federation, said: "Those who have reaped the benefits of globalization are increasingly afflicted by what has been called 'affluenza.' This condition distorts the values of life in fundamental ways, often leading to relativization of human dignity."

Meanwhile, mainline denominations in the United States continued to press for revisions in the president's proposed federal budget for 2006, which Episcopal presiding bishop Frank Griswold called unjust earlier this year.

Following Hurricane Katrina, "It is clear that greater burdens on these programs such as Medicaid and the food stamp program will occur," said John Johnson, domestic policy analyst in the Episcopal Church's Office of Government Relations. "Congress must...recommit itself to the values that Americans share in standing up for the poor and disenfranchised in our country.

Upping the Minimum Wage

Cliff Hocker

Businesses surviving on slim profit margins have another uncertainty to factor in to bottom-line projections. The U.S. Senate is expected to vote on legislation sponsored by Sen. Edward M. Kennedy (D-Mass.) that would raise the federal minimum wage from $5.15 per hour to $5.85 within 60 days of passage of the bill, then increase to $6.45 by 2005 and $7 by 2006. It would be the first minimum wage hike since 1997, affecting an estimated 7.4 million workers.

Routine increases in the minimum wage help alleviate discrimination against women and minorities, according to the Economic Policy Institute. Still, organizations such as the U.S. Chamber of Commerce and National Federation of Independent Business Owners continue to lobby against wage hikes, arguing that hikes increase the cost of doing business. Service sectors such as restaurants and hotels, where lower-paying jobs abound, are likely to feel the most heat.

The fast-food industry has entry-level positions where inexperienced youth develop job skills. Minimum wage increases will cramp a restaurant's ability to "over hire" to compensate for the inefficiencies of this training mode, says Valerie Daniels-Carter, founder and CEO of Milwaukee-based V&J Holding Co. Inc. (No. 38 on the BE INDUSTRIAL/SERVICE 100 list with $90 million in sales). V&J has very low turnover of its 3,500 Burger King and Pizza Hut staff. "We won't feel the shock the same way as a smaller operator that...has been in business for only a few years. You have enough small businesses that are on the bubble anyway, and for them to try to absorb a 35% increase in their labor line really is going to cause some businesses to fall out," says Daniels-Carter.

Jim Manly, Sen. Kennedy's press secretary, says 11 million new jobs were added after the last minimum wage increase. "History shows that raising the minimum wage has not had any negative effect on jobs, employment, or inflation," he adds. To the contrary, the Employment Policies Institute reports that 645,000 low-paying entry-level jobs were lost as a result of the 50 cent wage hike in 1996.

Cecelia A. Conrad, a member of *Black Enterprise* Board of Economists and an economics professor at Pomona College in Claremont, California, says any negative effects of minimum wage increase would be small. She anticipates little or no job loss and only slight price rises. "We have to sort of balance those against the potential positive benefits in terms of improvements in the standard of living for working families, particularly those headed by single mothers, which are the group that tends to benefit from minimum wage increases," says Conrad. "If a business is located in an inner-city community, there really is a kind of trade-off for them between potentially higher costs, but also customers with more dollars to spend."

Exercise 19, Essays on Image, Beauty, and Aging in America

Mirror, Mirror on the Wall…Are Muscular Men the Best of All?

Nancy Clark

Muscle dysmorphia is a new syndrome emerging behind gym doors. You might notice it in your gym's workout room. Some weight-lifters pathologically believe their muscles are too small. They have poor body image (i.e. are ashamed of, embarrassed by, and unhappy with their bodies) and a passionate desire not only to build muscle, but also avoid gaining fat. This preoccupation with building muscles manifests itself in excessive weightlifting (e.g., spending four or more hours per day at the gym), attention to diet (e.g. consuming protein shakes on a rigid schedule), time spent "body-checking" (e.g. looking in mirrors, CDs, window reflections, etc.), excessively weighing themselves (i.e. 10 to 20 times per day), too little time spent with family and friends and, not uncommonly, anabolic steroid use.

Is this overconcern with body size a new obsession? Perhaps. In the past few years, we have been increasingly exposed to half-naked, muscular male bodies (e.g. Calvin Klein underwear ads). Evidently, even brief exposure to these images can affect a man's view of

"Mirror, Mirror On The Wall… Are Muscular Men the Best of All?" – From *American Fitness, January/February 2004* by Nancy Clark. Reprinted by permission.

his body. In a study of the media's effect on male body image, a group of college men viewed advertisements featuring muscular men, while another group viewed neutral advertisements without partially naked male bodies. Then the men (unaware of the hypothesis being tested) were given a body image assessment. Those exposed to the muscular images showed a significantly greater discrepancy between the body they want to have and their current body size (Leit, Gray, and Pope 2002). Another study suggests up to a third of teenage boys are trying to gain weight to be stronger, fitter, attain a better body image, and perform better in sports (O'Dea and Rawstone 2001).

The irony is while college-age men believe a larger physique is more attractive to the opposite sex, women report desiring a normal-sized body. In a study of men from the United States, Austria, and France, the subjects were shown a spectrum of body images and asked to choose:

- the body they felt represented their own
- the body they would really like to have
- the body of an average man their age, and
- the male they felt women preferred.

The men chose an ideal male body that was about 28 pounds more muscular than their current bodies. They also reported believing women prefer a male body 30 pounds more muscular than they currently possessed. Yet, an accompanying study indicated women actually preferred an ordinary male body without added muscle (Pope 2000).

At the 2003 Massachusetts Eating Disorders Association's (MEDA) annual conference, Dr. Roberto Olivardia shared his research on adolescent boys' body image. Olivardia is a psychology instructor at Harvard Medical School and co-author of *The Adonis Complex: The Secret Crisis of Male Body Obsession* (Free Press, 2000). The title alludes to Adonis, the Greek god who exemplifies ideal masculine beauty and desire of all women. Olivardia explained that adolescence is a time for exploring "Who am I?" Without a doubt, so much of who a teen is, is defined by his body. Because today's boys have been exposed from day one to GI Joe action figures, Hulk Hogan, and Nintendo's Duke Nukem, they have relentlessly received strong messages that muscular bodies are desirable. Those at risk for muscle dysmorphia include adolescent boys who were teased as children about being too fat or short. Individuals at highest risk are those who base their self-esteem solely on their appearance.

In our society, muscularity is commonly associated with masculinity. According to Olivardia, compared to ordinary men, muscular men tend to command more respect and are deemed more powerful, threatening, and sexually virile. Muscular men perceive others as "backing off" and "taking them seriously." Not surprisingly, men's desire for muscles has manifested itself in a dramatic increase in muscle (and penile) implants.

Olivardia expressed concern the "bigger is better" mindset can often lead to anabolic steroid use. He cited statistics from a study with 3,400 high school male seniors: 6.6 percent reported having used steroids; more than two-thirds of that group started before age sixteen (Buckley et al. 1988). Olivardia regrets males commonly use steroids in secrecy and shame. "Men will tell someone they use cocaine before they admit to using 'juice.'" This commonly keeps them from seeking help.

Steroids carry with them serious medical concerns: breast enlargement, impotence, ache, mood swings, risk of heart disease, prostate cancer, liver damage, and AIDS (from sharing needles)—not to mention sudden death, although it may occur twenty years from current use. "Roid Rage," the fierce temper that contributes to brutal murders and violence against women, is an immediate danger.

What's the solution? According to Olivardia, young men need education about realistic body size to correct the distorted thought "if some muscle is good, then more muscle must be better." They might also need treatment for obsessive-compulsive disorder. Sadly, most men believe they are the only ones with this problem and, thereby, take a long time to admit needing therapy. When they do, too few programs exist to help them explore the function this obsession serves in their daily lives—a sense of control. They mistakenly believe control over their bodies equates to control over their lives.

My Cat Takes More Drugs Than I Do

Thomas Withers

Ironically, if I hadn't been trying to beat the high cost of health care, my wife wouldn't have run over my head with her bicycle a few months ago. The wheels on my bike hit a slick spot and I fell directly in her path. Missing me was impossible. Moments later I was sitting in the middle of the trail wearing a cracked helmet and saying, "What happened?"

Just before we'd begun our ride, my wife had looked at me and given me an angry ultimatum: "You are 86 years old, and if you don't know enough to wear your helmet, you can ride alone." Rue Ann is 29 years younger and more verbal than I, so I replied with resignation, "Yes dear," and donned my helmet.

How does the high cost of health care relate to my accident? It's simple. One of my strategies for avoiding health-care costs is to stay healthy, and that means riding regularly.

My plan works primarily for people in the 40- to 60-year age range, those young enough to make the necessary changes for entering old age with good health and enthusiasm. In towns like mine across the country, that's just not happening, and the result is that fewer people my age are still leading active lives.

Our local hospital, St. John's, will hold its 26th annual 10-kilometer foot race in October. About 2,000 people are expected to participate, but if it's anything like past years, I won't have much competition. Usually after a race, when people ask how well I did, I say, "I came in first in the 80- to 90-year-old class." Invariably, they ask the follow-up question, "How many were in that class?" With feigned embarrassment, I answer, "I was the only one."

My quest to see how little I could spend on health care began when I was 50. Two events spurred me to action: First, my blood pressure began rising above the normal range. Second, a close friend only a few years older than I had had a stroke that left him speechless, in diapers and in a nursing home. It also left him penniless.

In a society where health-care costs were spiraling out of control, how could I escape a similar fate? To protect myself, I considered many plans, from trying to marry a rich widow to buying long-term medical insurance. Finally, I thought of a strategy that would work, though the method I chose is somewhat un-American. I decided to take care of my health. It was the best decision I ever made.

The success of my plan lies in its simplicity. It's available and adaptable to almost everyone. Furthermore, it requires little special equipment other than a bicycle—and a helmet. The system I have followed for 37 years has three essential parts: nutrition, exercise and perseverance. Nutritionally, I deviate little from the U.S. Department of Agriculture's guidelines. All the foods needed to meet its requirements are available in a traditional food store. I head to the produce department to buy fresh fruits and vegetables to supplement those I grow in my garden. I read labels and put back products that are loaded with hydrogenated fats and sodium. When using these criteria, three fourths of the grocery aisles become irrelevant. As a result, my shopping is streamlined.

Rue Ann and I, depending on the weather, do one of the following five days a week: ride our bicycles 10 miles, walk 3 miles or climb the stairs in a 10-story building. Consistency is the key to a successful exercise program.

The financial payoff for this kind of living has exceeded my wildest expectations. I get a routine physical once a year. Intermittently, I see a dermatologist and ophthalmologist. When I was 75 my doctor said, "I know you don't take any prescription drugs, but what over-the-counter drugs do you take?" When I answered "None," he smiled and wryly said I wasn't doing my part to support the drug companies. Today my old cat's drug bill is higher than mine. I'm not sure if I'm bragging or complaining.

My biggest payoff, however, is not in the money I save, but in the way I feel. Now, just after my 87th birthday, I can still say "What's a headache? Constipation? Arthritis?" When I'm in the drug department of a supermarket, I feel like the bewildered Texas cowboy in a Dallas department store. When the clerk asked, "Is there something wrong?" I drawled, "No ma'am, I've just never seen so many things in my whole life I don't need."

Recently, as my wife and I were going through airport security, a young male employee said, "It sure is a nice weekend for a father-daughter outing." With a grin broader than natural, I replied, "It certainly is, and we are going to make the most of it—aren't we, daughter?"

I'm saving my cracked helmet with the bicycle-tire marks on it as a token of my good health. I hope I'm still wearing a helmet at 95, because the alternatives are unacceptable.

Putting Your Best Face Forward

Carl Elliot

If a team of alien anthropologists were looking for clues to understand the habits and sensibilities of 21st century Americans, it could start with the new Fox reality show, *The Swan*. Like *Extreme Makeover*, its predecessor on ABC, *The Swan* invites guests to undergo dramatic self-transformations with the help of fitness trainers, hair stylists, makeup consultants and cosmetic surgeons. Unlike the guests on *Extreme Makeover*, however, contestants on *The Swan* will be prevented from seeing how their cosmetic surgery has turned out until the season finale. In the episode, called "The Ultimate Swan Pageant," 18 surgically altered finalists will compete against one another in a televised, two-hour beauty contest. For the anthropologist, here is an artifact that promises to combine some of the most significant aspects of contemporary American life: grueling competition, the possibility of extreme social humiliation, and plenty of women in bathing suits.

The fact that so many people eagerly undergo such dramatic procedures (and that millions of people watch them do it) suggests that something deeper is at work here. In fact, the desire for self-transformation has been a part of American life since the earliest days of the republic. How many other countries can count a best-selling self-help author such as Benjamin Franklin among their founding fathers? Cosmetic surgery, once a slightly shameful activity, is now performed at elite medical institutions such as the Mayo Clinic and John Hopkins University. According to the American Society of Aesthetic Plastic Surgery,

Americans underwent 8.3 million cosmetic medical procedures in 2003. That figure represents a 20 percent increase from the previous year and a 293 percent increase since 1997.

At the beginning of the 20th century, sociologist Charles Cooley described the American identity as a "looking-glass self." Our sense of ourselves, wrote Cooley, is formed by our imagination of the way we appear in the eyes of others. Other people are a looking glass in which we see not merely our own reflection but a judgment about the value of that reflection. ("Each to each a looking glass/Reflects the other that doth pass," he wrote.) If we are lucky, we feel pride in that imagined self; if not, we feel mortification.

The metaphor of the looking glass suggests Narcissus, bewitched by his own image, but Cooley did not think that we are entirely self-centered. As he pointed out, we are often keenly aware of the characteristics of the people in whose minds we imagine ourselves. We are more self-conscious about our looks in the presence of the brave. But in the end, when we gaze into the looking glass, we are interested in the reflections mainly because they are ours. "Enough about me," as the old joke goes. "What do *you* think about me?"

In fact, there is a sense in which Cooley's looking-glass self is built right into our moral system. The moral ideal at work here is "recognition." As the philosopher Charles Taylor has written, today we feel it is crucially important to be recognized and respected for who we are. This has not always been the case. The desire for recognition is not as important in times or places in which identity is considered immutable and predetermined—where it is a part of a social hierarchy. We find recognition so important today precisely because so many aspects of our identities are neither immutable nor predetermined. We are not simply born into a caste or social role. We are expected to build an individual identity for ourselves by virtue of how we live and the way we present ourselves to others. Manners, accent, clothes, hair, job, home, even personality: All are now seen as objects of individual control that express something important about who we are.

But building a successful identity cannot be done in isolation. It depends on the recognition of others. And that recognition can be withheld. (You can insist you are a woman, for example, while others insist that you are really a man.) Sometimes recognition can be given, yet given in a way that demeans the person being recognized. It's no surprise that from its inception, cosmetic surgery has been enthusiastically employed to efface markers of ethnicity, such as the "Jewish nose" or "Asian eyes." Recognition is necessary for self-respect, and if it is denied, as W.E.B. DuBois famously put it, one is placed in the position of "measuring one's soul by the tape of the world that looks on in amused contempt and pity." Many Americans have given up on changing the world and have decided to change themselves instead.

Some people will see shows such as *Extreme Makeover* and *The Swan* as a kind of institutionalized cruelty. After all, they search for contestants whose special psychological vulnerability is an abiding shame about their personal appearance, and then offer them the chance for redemption only if they agree to appear on national television in their underwear. (A Fox vice president, sounding eerily like Nurse Ratched from *One Flew Over the Cuckoo's Nest,* adds that contestants will be put through "rigorous emotional and physical reconditioning.")

Yet there is something weirdly appropriate about cosmetic surgery winding up on television. This may be the logical endpoint of the looking-glass self. It is not just that people on television are on average much better looking than the rest of us, though that is certainly true. It is also that the average American spends four hours a day watching television. It would be surprising if all that viewing time did not make us more self-conscious. As the novelist David Foster Wallace puts it, four hours a day spent watching television means four hours a day of unconscious reinforcement that genuine human worth dwells in the phenomenon of being watched.

Exercise 21, Essays about Environmental Concerns in America

Once Unique, Soon a Place Like Any Other

Abe Whaley

I grew up in the mountains of East Tennessee, on a modest farm where we raised a lot of what we ate, watched sunsets on the porch and had supper together every night. For nine generations, mine included, both sides of my family have lived and died in the shadows of the surrounding peaks.

My formative years were spent listening to Papaw (my grandfather) saw away on an old fiddle and Dad flat-pick his six-string guitar as they taught me the songs of Southern Appalachia and handed down a centuries-old musical tradition. A great-great-great-great-great-grandfather of mine was baptized into the Forks of the Pigeon River Baptist Church in 1796, which he later pastored for 31 years—we are still faithful members, though the name has changed. No one ever really moves away from here and no one ever used to move in. Lately, though, they've been coming in droves.

The Great Smoky Mountains National Park, where my family lived before 1933, and Dollywood, Dolly Parton's theme park, draw year-round crowds. New home construction has been climbing steadily for years, and the rental housing market, mostly overnight log-cabin outfits, has exploded. It seems that no ridge is too steep, no mountaintop too high, no creek too pristine to bulldoze and build on.

I haven't been home much since I graduated from high school six years ago. College, a "real" job, extended international travel, the Tennessee Air National Guard, and work on a master's degree have kept me pretty busy. As much as I love visiting, I hate the trip back. Every time I drive the road into town I see more ridges in the distance that have fallen to construction.

Do not misunderstand me, it is not the simple single-family homes that are so irritating; I have framed up quite a few of those over my summer breaks from school. What bothers me is the way developers feel the need to put a subdivision on the most beautiful piece of mountain farmland they can find. Of course, the farmers cannot be blamed much— a million-dollar buyout sounds a lot better than trying to make ends meet for another 20 harvests and then losing it all to the bank during their retirement years. But the land magnates, most of whom are from out of town, have no excuse. They wreak wholesale destruction on the surrounding mountaintops and ridgelines as they build their rental cabins and condominiums. They ruin the views that make our piece of Southern Appalachia so enviable in the first place.

I traveled extensively in New Zealand last year and I was amazed by the environmental ethos that seems to be shared by its government and citizens. I rarely saw mass development that went higher than halfway up the mountains that surrounded any given town. The locals I talked to told me that most places had laws that limited construction. What a novel idea—to zone in such a way as to minimize the environmental havoc that developers can impose. Our planners and decision makers could use a lesson in that kind of logic. But so often government officials seem more interested in privately investing in land deals than publicly regulating them.

Those of us seeking to preserve the countryside in Tennessee were dealt another blow by the Supreme Court's recent decision in *Kelo v. City of New London.* The court upheld the government's power of eminent domain, which allows it to take private land for public purpose. Unfortunately, the court ruled that public purpose can be interpreted as economic growth. The chairman of the Tennessee Valley Authority, which acquired most of its waterfront property through eminent domain years ago, has already stated that the fate of 181,000 acres of wild land set aside for natural-resource conservation is negotiable. This has developers licking their lips in anticipation as they dream of building houses on top of hiking trails. It is obvious that nothing is sacred. It scares me. It scares me a lot.

Though native Appalachians like me are gradually being outnumbered by newcomers, we remain tied to the land in a way outsiders will never understand. It provides for us physically, socially, spiritually and emotionally. Without it, we lose our cultural identity and, ultimately, ourselves. This is not a new fight; it has raged in these mountains for generations as our land has been exploited again and again. For too long, we have

123

suffered the effects of clear-cutting, strip mining and unscrupulous land grabs by timber companies, coal companies and even the federal government. Developers are simply the latest to try their hand at making a buck.

My home is fast becoming a place like many others in this country, homogenized and prepackaged. My roots are neither of those things, and the land I grew up on deserves something better than the reckless development now disgracing its rugged beauty.

Sample Bibliographic Essays

The Myth of the American Dream

Laura Grow

The 'American dream' is a term coined by James Truslow Adams in his 1931 book *Epic of America*, but it is a concept as old as America itself: anything is possible if only the individual is willing to work hard. The dream draws immigrants to our shores and borders every year and keeps millions of Americans content in the notion that their toiling will pave the way to prosperity for them and for their children. However, for every rags-to-riches story, there are thousands of other hard-working people who cannot get by, who don't have enough to eat, transportation, safe housing, or warm clothes in winter. There is much evidence that the American dream is little more than a myth, a false promise that keeps millions of people working themselves weary for a better tomorrow that will never come.

Historical Perspectives

The American dream is the promise of the Declaration of Independence, which indicates that our "inalienable rights" are "life, liberty, and the pursuit of happiness." There is no single American dream, but the concept is defined by Adams in its noblest sense:

> [It is the] dream of a land in which life should be better and richer and fuller for everyone, with opportunity for each according to ability or achievement...a dream of a social order in which each man and each woman shall be able to attain to the fullest stature of which they are innately capable, and be recognized by others for what they are, regardless of the fortuitous circumstances of birth or position. (qtd. in Ferenza)

The lure of America for immigrants and the promise to its citizens is that, as Adams indicates, the individual is not restrained by circumstances, but through individual efforts can pursue and attain whatever personal brand of happiness he or she desires.

In the wake of the Great Depression, Franklin Roosevelt recognized the part the federal government needed to play in keeping the American dream alive—no longer was hard work the only factor involved in ensuring an acceptable standard of living. Under his administration, a number of social programs were put into place to help Americans achieve the dream, which Roosevelt described as "sufficiency of life, rather than…a plethora of riches [and] good health, good food, good education, good working conditions" (qtd. in Muir). Owing to these principles, Roosevelt's New Deal included the Social Security Act, Fair Labor Standards Act that banned child labor and established a minimum wage, and a variety of programs that put Americans to work in civil service ("Successes"). Roosevelt's programs and World War II helped drag the nation out of the Great Depression, but were not permanent solutions in making the American dream possible for all Americans.

By the 1960s, one in five Americans were living in poverty, and in his first State of the Union address in 1964, Lyndon Johnson, echoing the sentiments of his predecessor Roosevelt, declared "an unconditional war on poverty in America" (qtd. in Quindlen "The War"). Johnson, too, understood that the American dream was one not attainable through hard work alone. As Anna Quindlen, Pulitzer-prize winning journalist, notes in her 2004 editorial "The War We Haven't Won," "from [Johnson's] declaration a host of government initiatives sprang, including Head Start, an expanded food-stamp program, and sweeping reforms in health care for the needy."

Unfortunately, in spite of the attempts of Roosevelt, Johnson, and others to lend a hand to those Americans who need it most, the sentiment that the impoverished are responsible for their own plight always seems to creep its way back into the American consciousness. We've all heard the grumblings that the poor are lazy, that welfare is just an excuse not to get a job. Quindlen comments that "part of the problem with a war on poverty today is that many Americans have decided that being poor is a character defect, not an economic condition." Public policy of the last few decades seems to follow this line of thinking: the Federal minimum wage has not risen since 1997 even as welfare reform movements have forced millions of people, many single parents, off public assistance and into minimum wage jobs. Quindlen argues that "forty years after Johnson led the charge, the battle against poverty still rages. The biggest difference today is that there is no call to arms by those in power." How does this shift in American policy affect the status of the American dream? Can we still call ourselves the land of opportunity when the American dream eludes so many of our citizens?

The American Dream Today

In July 2000, Mortimer Zuckerman, editor-in-chief of *U.S. News and World Report*, wrote an essay lauding the success of the American dream. Zuckerman claims that "it is a dream built on individual effort—talent, ambition, risk-taking, readiness to change, and just plain hard work—qualities that count more in America than social background or luck."

That is a perspective that Zuckerman, a billionaire whose biography on the *U.S. News and World Report* website boasts he has "substantial real-estate holdings, including properties in Boston, New York, Washington, and San Francisco," can afford to have. The reality for most Americans, however, is not nearly so rosy. It is a reality where social background and luck play far too large a part in achieving the American dream.

Two articles written a decade apart demonstrate that bitter reality. In *USA Today* in 1996, Charles Whalen writes that "beneath the misleading surface prosperity [of the 1990s] are numerous alarming trends," among them "relentless downsizing," "longer job searches and sluggish job creation," "explosive growth in contingent work" (part-time and temporary employment), and "wage stagnation." One would be hard-pressed to find a list that better demonstrates the part luck plays in securing steady employment. Whalen also cites a survey, ironically conducted for *U.S. News and World Report*, that indicates "57% of those asked said that the American dream is out of reach for most families."

In 2006 in the Chicago Sun-Times, Clyde Murphy cites a "new report released by the Opportunity Agenda [that] measures the nation's progress in living up to the American dream." The findings? That "millions of Americans do not have a fair chance to achieve their full potential, despite their best efforts." Two of the reasons cited by the study are housing discrimination against blacks, Hispanics, and Asians and employment discrimination against women and minorities, which included favoring job candidates with "white-sounding" names. These findings clearly refute Zuckerman's claim, demonstrating that background does in fact "count more in America" than "individual effort" when it comes to achieving certain aspects of the American dream.

Another dubious claim in Zuckerman's essay is that "anybody who wishes to work has the opportunity to move from the bottom of the ladder to a middle-class standard of life, or higher." As award-winning journalist Barbara Ehrenreich notes in her book *Nickel and Dimed: On (Not) Getting By in America*, the rhetoric surrounding welfare reform "assumed that a job was the ticket out of poverty and that the only thing holding back welfare recipients was their reluctance to get out and get one" (196). As a wealth of evidence suggests, this is the fundamental misperception surrounding the American dream.

In her 2003 editorial "A New Kind of Poverty," Anna Quindlen argues that "America is a country that now sits atop a precarious latticework of myth. It is the myth that working people can support their families." Quindlen interviews two women who run services for the homeless and impoverished in New York City, and they note that more often they are seeing working families in dire need of their help. Indeed, according to the U.S. Census Bureau's 2005 report on poverty, America's poverty rate has been climbing, from 11.3 percent in 2000 to 12.7 percent in 2004, the latest year for which data is available. This translates into 37 million people who live below the poverty line. This is further complicated, however, by the way that the Census Bureau calculates the poverty level. Barbara Ehrenreich explains that "[it] is still calculated by the archaic method of taking the bare-bones cost of food for a family of a given size and multiplying that number by three. Yet food is relatively inflation-proof" (200). This method results in a base calculation of $9,310 for one person, with $3,180 added for each additional person in the household. As anyone who has ever lived on his or her own understands, those poverty calculations are very low. Ehrenreich points out that "the Economic Policy Institute recently reviewed dozens of studies of what constitutes a 'living wage' and came up with an average figure of $30,000 for a family of one adult and two children" (213). When compared to the federal poverty calculation of $15,670, the gap becomes glaringly apparent. Anna Quindlen explains "when you adjust the level to reflect reality, you come closer to 35 percent of all Americans who are having a hard time providing the basics for their families" ("The War").

As pioneering psychologist Abraham Maslow's research reveals, physiological and safety needs—the "basics" referred to by Quindlen, such as food and housing—must be fulfilled before other needs, core components of the American dream such as belongingness and self-esteem, can be met ("Abraham"). This creates a basic gap between those who can reach for the American dream and those who can't; if all someone's energy is focused on providing food and shelter, there is nothing left to reach for higher goals. In a 2002 essay "What's So Great About America?" Dinesh D'Souza, an Indian immigrant, makes assertions that demonstrate some common misperceptions about Americans meeting our basic needs. "The United States is a country where the ordinary guy has a good life," according to D'Souza. He even goes so far as to say that "very few people in America have to wonder where their next meal is coming from" (23). Sadly, this is not true. Quindlen indicates "the U.S. Department of Agriculture notes that 1.6 million New Yorkers...suffer from 'food insecurity,' which is just a fancy way of saying they don't have enough to eat" ("A New"). Ehrenreich reports that "according to a survey conducted by the U.S. Conference of Mayors, 67 percent of the adults requesting emergency food aid are people with jobs" (219).

Two other basic needs, safe housing and health care, are also beyond the reach of many Americans. "When the rich and the poor compete for housing on the open market," writes Ehrenreich, "the poor don't stand a chance. The rich can always outbid them, buy up their tenements and trailer parks, and replace them with...whatever they like" (199). This is exacerbated by the fact that "expenditures on public housing have fallen since the 1980s, and the expansion of public rental subsidies came to a halt in the 1990s" (Ehrenreich 201). Health care is another sad story. According to the U.S. Census Bureau, the number of Americans with no health insurance has been slowly rising, arriving at 15.7 percent in 2004, and as Quindlen observes, "poor kids are much more likely to become sick than their counterparts, but much less likely to have health insurance. Talk about a double whammy" ("The War"). How can families dream big and plan for the future as they worry about whether the next month will bring eviction or illness?

Two people in particular have put a human face on the statistical evidence that the American dream remains out of reach for millions of hard-working Americans. At the urging of her editor at *Harper's* magazine, Barbara Ehrenreich undertook a year-long undercover investigation of living on low-wage jobs in Florida, Maine, and Minnesota. She waited tables, worked as a maid, and worked at Wal-Mart, never revealing her status as a reporter, but keeping careful private diaries documenting the details of her experience. In spite of working at least full-time, usually more, she was unable to get by. The most heartbreaking part of her journey, however, was the people she met, women who were not just experimenting with the low-wage life, but who were trapped by it. They were women who were victims of the affordable housing shortage, who lived in cars, or if they were lucky, weekly rental motel rooms. They walked, rode bikes, or bummed rides to work. Certainly among those who experience "food insecurity," they skipped meals or ate nutritionally void foods like hot dog buns because they couldn't afford to eat. They were women with raw hands and sore backs, tenuously balancing two or more jobs who would never, in spite of their work ethic, move off that bottom rung of the social ladder.

In a similar experiment, Morgan Spurlock (of *Super Size Me* fame) and his fiancée lived on minimum wage for thirty days in Columbus, Ohio and recorded the results for the premiere episode of his television series *30 Days*. As Spurlock works eighteen-hour days making at least $7.50 per hour and Alex works for minimum wage at a coffee house, the pair is faced with a host of challenges that mirror the everyday trials of the working poor. Emergency room visits for a urinary tract infection and a sprained wrist cost them $1,217. D'Souza correctly comments that in America, "even sick people who don't have money or insurance will receive medical care at hospital emergency rooms" (23), but he fails to take into account that such care generates bills that are unmanageable for low-wage workers. Spurlock's and Alex's hospital bills are equivalent to six weeks' of full time minimum wage work. The most affordable housing they could find, a steal at $325 per month, has ant infestations, malfunctioning heat, and is upstairs from an apartment that was a crack house just the week before. Furthermore, their relationship is strained by the stress that results from the constant worrying about money. At the end of the month they find themselves hundreds of dollars in the hole, but permanently changed by their experience. When taken together, the accounts of Ehrenreich and Spurlock offer powerful insight into the everyday struggles of the working poor, those who are anything but lazy but still find themselves drowning financially, the American dream slipping further away all the time.

Final Thoughts

Dinesh D'Souza claims that "in America your destiny is not prescribed. Your life is like a blank sheet of paper and you are the artist" (24). It is difficult to believe, however, that the millions of working poor are not trying to create a better destiny for themselves, only to find their dreams thwarted by the harsh realities of daily life. So why is the American dream still such a pervasive part of our consciousness, even in the face of overwhelming evidence that hard work is not the ticket to prosperity, or even necessarily to a comfortable standard of living?

In his "Critique of Hegel's Philosophy of the Right," Karl Marx wrote that "religion is the sigh of the oppressed creature, the heart of a heartless world, just as it is the spirit of a spiritless situation. It is the opium of the people. The abolition of religion as the illusory happiness of the people is required for their real happiness" (qtd. in Cline). Marx's astute observation is that religion, in keeping the focus on the afterlife, keeps people from demanding fair treatment in this world. D'Souza suggests, however, that "capitalism gives America a this-worldly focus that allows death and the afterlife to recede from everyday view...the gaze of the people is shifted to earthly progress" (25). If this is the case, why is it that we are not more cognizant of (and enraged about!) the decided lack of "earthly progress" of so many of our friends and neighbors? I believe that it is because the American dream has taken the place of religion as today's "opiate of the masses." So long as we all believe that there is a better life ahead, that if we only work harder, our dreams are within reach, it is easy to be lulled into complacency about the inequality that is so prevalent in America today. Barbara Ehrenreich predicts that someday the working poor "are bound to tire of getting so little in return [for their labor] and to demand to be paid what they're worth" (221). I contend, echoing Marx, that Ehrenreich's prediction will not come true until the American dream, "the illusory happiness of the people," is abolished in favor of a more realistic world view that recognizes that more than hard work, a helping hand is needed to make America truly the land of opportunity. [2,755 words]

Works Cited

"Abraham Maslow's Hierarchy of Needs." *Shippensberg University Website.* Sept. 2005. <http://www.ship.edu/~cgboeree/maslow.html>.

Cline, Austin. "Karl Marx on Religion." *About.com.* 5 Apr. 2006. <http://atheism.about.com/od/weeklyquotes/a/marx01.htm>.

D'Souza, Dinesh. "What's So Great About America?" *The American Enterprise.* Apr./May 2002: 22-25.

Ehrenreich, Barbara. *Nickel and Dimed: On (Not) Getting By in America.* New York: Owl Books, 2002.

Ferenz, Kathleen. "What is the American Dream?" *San Francisco State University Online Web Site.* 31 Mar. 2005. <http://online.sfsu.edu/~kferenz/syllabus/dreams/thedream.html>.

Hawksley, Humphrey. "The Stark Reality of the American Dream." *BBC News Web Site.* 31 Mar. 2006. <http://newsvote.bbc.co.uk>.

"Minimum Wage." Writ. Penn Jillette Teller, Star Price, John McLaughlin, Jon Hotchkiss, Emma Webster, Jonathan Taylor, David Wechter, Michael Goudeau. Dir. Star Price. FX Network. 2005.

"Mortimer Zuckerman Editorial Columns." *U.S. News and World Report Website.* 5 Apr. 2006. <http://www.usnews.com/usnews/opinion/mzuckerman.htm>.

Muir, Ed. "Narrowing the Highway to the American Dream." *American Teacher.* Oct. 2004. 25.

Murphy, Clyde. "When Opportunity Knocks, It Skips Over Some Addresses." *Chicago Sun-Times.* 14 Feb. 2006: 33.

Quindlen, Anna. "A New Kind of Poverty." *Newsweek.* 1 Dec. 2003: 76.

____. "The War We Haven't Won." *Newsweek.* 20 Sep. 2004: 64.

"Successes and Failures of Roosevelt's 'New Deal' Programs." *Bergen County Technical Schools and Special Services Web Site.* 10 Mar. 2006. 5 Apr. 2006.
    <http://www.bergen.org/AAST/Projects/depression/ successes.html>.
U.S. Census Bureau. *2005 Poverty Press Release.* 30 Aug. 2005. 5 Apr. 2006.
    <http://www.census.gov/Press-
    Release/www/releases/archives/income_wealth/005647.html>.
U.S. Department of Health and Human Services. *2004 HHS Poverty Guidelines.* 13 Feb. 2004. 5. Apr.
    2006. < http://aspe.hhs.gov/poverty/04poverty.shtml>.
Whalen, Charles J. "The Age of Anxiety: Erosion of the American Dream." *USA Today.* Sep. 1996: 14-16.
Zuckerman, Mortimer. "A Time to Celebrate." *U.S. News and World Report.* 17 Jul. 2000: 120.

The next two examples have both strengths *and* weaknesses, which your instructor will discuss with you. The first has several problems with source citation. See if you can find them!

The Video Game War

Robert Klenk and Emanuele Solito

Thomas Storck, prominent author and contributing editor of the New Oxford Review, defines censorship as "the restriction, absolute, or merely to some part of the population (e.g., to the unlearned or to children), by the proper political authorities, of intellectual, literary, or artistic material in any format" (18). This definition will be used hereafter to shed light on the controversy that surrounds the video game industry. The Bill of Rights is designed to defend our civil liberties, but we will investigate the question of whether ratings systems and regulatory agencies pose a threat to our basic right to free speech. In recent years, the video game industry has been under pressure by the government to regulate the content of video games, and at the same time the Federal Communications Commission (FCC) regulates television, music, and radio. Ultimately, it is clear that ratings boards are a good way for the video game industry to regulate itself without the government interfering, but the FCC infringes on the First Amendment rights by fining broadcasters because of their content.

History of Video Game Rating Boards and the FCC

During the 1980s Nintendo dominated the video game market. Its Nintendo Entertainment System held both the American and Japanese Market, but there were different versions for each market because the Japanese Nintendo had content that was deemed inappropriate by American standards. Since American society is more socially conservative than Japan's, "Nintendo of America had come up with a series of polices and conventions regarding video game content that essentially became unquestioned the law of the land" ("Nintendo" 1). In other words, since Nintendo was the first, their standards for content became the norm.

The policies put in place by Nintendo are similar to those of the ratings boards of today. In the early 1990s, a few games came under the scrutiny of some key political officials. They felt that games like *Doom* were too violent for the youth of the day to handle. This put pressure on the video game industry to come up with an industry-wide rating system as a means of helping parents restrict access to inappropriate content for certain age groups. Thus the Entertainment System Rating Board (ESRB) was born. It modeled its guidelines after those of Nintendo. Lawrence Walters, a civil rights lawyer, writes that the ratings ranged from the child friendly "E for everyone" to "AO for adults only" (Walters "Video"). Ultimately, the video game industry took responsibility for monitoring its own content before the government got involved and regulated it for them.

On the other hand is the FCC, "an independent United States government agency, directly responsible to Congress" ("About"). According to the FCC website, the FCC "was established by the Communications Act of 1934 and is charged with regulating interstate and international communications by radio, television, wire, satellite and cable" ("About"). The FCC regulates these forms of communication by having set guidelines for decency and fining corporations when these guidelines are broken. The FCC feels that they need to regulate video games they deem too violent or aggressive for children to play, compared to the ESRB who feels that their purpose is to guide parents by rating the video games instead of just censoring them.

Ratings Boards vs. The FCC

Rating boards like the ESRB are designed to help parents monitor the kind of content that their children are exposed to. For parents who are not informed about the latest games coming out, the ESRB is there to step in and explain the type of game as well as the level of maturity that is needed to play the game. Adam Thierer, the director of Telecommunications Studies at the Cato Institute in Washington D.C., writes that the ratings system "applies five different rating symbols and over twenty-five different content labels that refer to violence, sex, language, substance abuse, gambling, humor and other potentially sensitive subject matter" (1). The ratings system makes it easier for parents to judge the content that their children are viewing. As Rabkin, a professor at Cornell University notes in his article "Do Kids Need Government Censorship?" "Although age-based ratings are not censorship, they can, with the cooperation of entertainment producers, retailers, and parents, effectively restrict the dissemination of offensive material to young people." As long as the parents are doing their part to monitor the games their child are playing, then the ESRB is effective in that it keeps the First Amendment from being trampled by outside forces censoring video game content. As lawyer Lawrence Walters asserts in his interview with GameAttorneys.com, "it is important to understand that

131

restrictions by private companies do not constitute censorship in the legal sense. In order for censorship to occur, the government must be directly involved." Walters's observation clearly points out the difference between the function the ESRB serves and the unconstitutional function of the FCC.

Since the FCC is a government entity, it clearly has no right to step in and regulate television and radio content. In another article by Adam Thierer called "Surrogate-Parent Sam," he indicates that he has "a serious problem with calling in Uncle Sam to play the role of a surrogate parent..." He thinks that the FCC has gone too far in regulating what is good and what is bad on the television, preferring instead that parents play censor to what their children hear and see. Mark Washburn, a well-known radio announcer for the *Charlotte Observer*, agrees with Thierer in his recent article "FCC Fines Set Limits" that the FCC has gone too far in defining what broadcasters can get away with on television and radio. Thierer and Washburn are part of the growing contingency that believes the FCC has too much power and is abusing the First Amendment. On the other hand, Keith Geiger, former deputy assistant secretary of Academic Programs at the State Department and former president of the National Education Association, believes that after children watch television or play video games, they see violence as fun, think it's a way for them to solve their problems, and even sometimes believe that they will be rewarded for their actions. He claims that some children cannot establish a sense of real life consequences for actions taken in video games and that the FCC should step in and help the parents decide what is suitable for their child.

Television has changed a great deal since the days that Lucille Ball couldn't even use the word "pregnant" on *I Love Lucy*. It is a commonplace to see shows like *CSI* or *ER* vividly depicting blood and violence in living color and television and radio alike pushing the envelope in terms of language and sexual content, but ultimately it is right to "clean up" radio and television just so children won't see something "inappropriate"? In his article "Violence Censorship in the Media," Adam Thierer says it best when he states that "parents need to act responsibly and exercise their private right—indeed, responsibility—to censor their children's eyes and ears from certain things" (2). Every family has a different set of standards and values of what too violent and with the rating system a parent will be able to choose what is appropriate for their children rather than having the government choose for them.

The problem with the FCC is that parents don't get the chance to decide what is appropriate for their children, and this arm of the government is violating the First Amendment by imposing increasingly steep fines for violations of their strict guidelines. Max Robins, editor in chief of *Broadcasting and Cable* notes that "*Without a Trace*... got more than 100 CBS stations slapped with a total of $3.6 million in fines from the FCC" for sexual content that was deemed inappropriate by the FCC. Everyone remembers the Janet Jackson Super Bowl controversy from three years ago, which resulted in millions in fines for ABC.

This practice of fining and censorship is in direct contrast to how the ESRB operates; the ESRB allows video game designers to makes their own changes to their games if they want a more marketable rating. For example Robin Raskin, former editor of *PC Magazine*, reports "there'll be negotiations for ratings: 'If I can change the bloodcurdling screams...will that take care of our little problem?'" Even though this may be a simple way of putting it, it demonstrates that game designers are not forced to change their work, but that they can choose to negotiate with the ratings board if they want a product marketable to younger audiences. The ESRB allows for such things to happen, while the FCC does not bend; if broadcasting companies cross the line, even through no fault of their own as in the Janet Jackson debacle, they face serious repercussions from the FCC.

There are still those, however, who believe there should be more oversight of the ESRB in regulating the content of video games. According to the U.S. Senate website, Senators Hillary Clinton and Joe Lieberman are working to develop legislation that will take care of the problem of the violent and sexual content inside video games. They do not want to see underage children getting their hands on video games that are not suitable, so they introduced the Family Entertainment Protection Act to Congress. This legislation will help keep adult-rated video games out of the hands of children. According to Troy Roberts of *Computer Games* magazine, "The Act is intended to keep mature rated video games from falling into the hands of children by fining the managers of retail outlets." Therefore, Senators Clinton and Lieberman prefer that the burden of responsibility lie with the retailers who sell video games, CDs, and DVDs, rather than with parents. This is much like how the FCC operates in forcing broadcasters to conform to "decency" standards rather than asking parents to monitor their children's entertainment.

The recent flood of legislation in Congress to regulate the sale of inappropriate content in video games has scared many retailers across the nation, causing them to perform their own form of censorship. As revealed in *Intellectual Freedom,* a journal published by the American Library Association, "...some large retailers, including Wal-Mart stores and Montgomery Ward, decided recently not to carry some violent video games, including, 'Doom,' 'Quake,' and 'South Park.'" However, not all retail chains feel the same way. For example, one company that does not buy into this system is Best Buy. Joy Harris, a well read author in advocating video games rating systems, said "We carry everything. We strongly encourage parents to review ratings [however] Best Buy does not consider itself in the business of censorship" ("Retailers"). Ultimately, it shouldn't be a store's place to censor the games that they sell because parents should take the responsibility to monitor their children's purchases.

Final Thoughts

When we approached the topic of censorship and video games, we were confused at first. After reading several articles on the topic we had a more broad idea what censoring video games is all about. In the end, we believe that the ESRB is doing a good enough job in taking care of the ratings of video games. It is the parents' responsibility to monitor what their children are playing and decide whether or not it is suitable for them. By having the government step in, it takes away responsibility from the parents in deciding what is right for their child. This is where the FCC went wrong because they are now just acting as censors of what is on television. We believe that the FCC should not be able to regulate what is on television because in doing so, they violate the First Amendment right to free speech. [1,945 words]

Works Cited

Alpert, Hollis. *Censorship: For & Against.* Ed. Harold H. Hart. Hart Publishing Company Inc., 1971. 10-24.

Federal Communication Commission. "About the FCC." 18 April, 2006. <http://www.fcc.gov/aboutus.html>.

Game Attorneys. 3 April, 2006. <http://www.gameattorneys.com>.

Geiger, Keith. "Profiting By Violence." *NEA Today.* 12.7 (Mar. 1994): 2.

Killian, Seth. "Violent Video Game Players Mysteriously Avoid Killing Selves, Others." *NCAC Censorship.* 4 April 2006. <http://www.ncac.org/censorship_news/20040121~cn092~Violent_Video_Game_Players_ Mysteriously_Avoid_Killing_Selves_-_Others.cfm>.

Kushner, David. "Sex, Lies, & Video Games. *Rolling Stone.* 11 Aug. 2005: 41-42.

"Nintendo's Era of Censorship." *Filibuster Cartoons.* 4 April 2006. <http://www.filibustercartoons.com/ Nintendo.php>.

Rabkin, Rhoda. "Do Kids Need Government Censors?" *Policy Review* (Mar. 2002): 27-42.

Rauch, Jonathan, and Salman Rushdie. "Censorship is Harmful." *Opposing Viewpoints: Censorship.* Ed. David Bender and Bruno Leone. San Diego: Greenhaven Press, 1997, 18-23.

"Retailers Drop Violent Video Games." *Intellectual Freedom* (Nov. 1999): 159.

Roberts, Troy. "Game-Restriction Bill Sent to Congress." *Computer Games* (Dec. 2005): 55.

Robins, Max. "Playing Dirty." *Broadcasting and Cable.* (Jan. 2004): 47-50.

"Senators Clinton, Lieberman Announce Federal Legislation to Protect Children from Inappropriate Video Games." *United States Senate.* 06 April 2006. <http://www.senate.gov/~clinton/news/statements/ details.cfm?id=249368>.

Storck, Thomas. "Censorship Can Be Beneficial." *Opposing Viewpoints: Censorship.* Eds. David Bender and Bruno Leone. Greenhaven Press, 1997, 18-23.

Thierer, Adam. "Censoring Violence in Media." *TechKnowledge.* 3 April 2006. <http://www.cato.org/tech/tk/040810-tk.html>.

---. "Regulating Video Games: Must Government Mind Our Children?" *TechKnowledge.* 3 April, 2006. <http://www.cato.org/tech/tk/030624-tk.html>.

---. "Surrogate-Parent Sam." *TechKnowledge.* 18 April 2006. <www.cato.org/tech/tk-index.html>.

Walters, Lawrence G. "Interview Regarding Video Games and the First Amendment."

---. "Video Game Industry Takes Aim At Censorship." *Game Attorneys.* 4 April 2006. <http://www.gameattorneys.com>.

The New Family

Kelly Dermyer and Becky DeMars

The American family is traditionally seen as a mother/father/child combination. The media has reinforced these traditional views about how families should be structured through shows like *The Adventures of Ozzie and Harriet, Leave it to Beaver,* and *7th Heaven.* While this kind of family make-up is true for some, fewer traditional families exist today due to changes in society, and some people question if the "traditional" family ever really existed in the first place. American families are increasingly made up of a single-parent with children, two working parents with children, or other combinations where extended relatives or foster parents play a part. Many people believe that this break-down of the traditional family structure is at the center of society's problems today. However, most evidence suggests that this is not the case. Families that deviate from the norm of family structure are not the basis of society's problems.

Til Death Do Us Part?

From the beginning, marriage has been the binding of a man and a woman for life. According to R. Claire Snyder, associate professor in the Department of Public and International Affairs at George Mason University, "Man and woman are naturally different, designed by God for heterosexual marriage and the establishment of the patriarchal family" (285). From this viewpoint, the family should be composed of a man and a woman forever and always. With these arguments supporting traditional marriages it is hard to believe that families of different types are just as beneficial to society and even more widespread. Doctor Shere Hite, a social researcher and cultural historian, refutes the primacy of traditional marriages when she writes:

> There is a positive new diversity springing up in families and relationships today in Western society. This pluralism should be valued and encouraged: far from signaling a breakdown of society, it is a sign of a new, more open and tolerant society springing up, a new world being born out of the clutter of the old. (26-27)

Hite's perspective demonstrates that different kinds of families are just as effective and normal as traditional families. Neither Hite nor Snyder is blatantly incorrect in their views on families; However, Snyder is blinded by stereotypes. Changing families are not necessarily bad for society; they are just new and different. Without giving the changes a chance, we will not know whether or not society could be better.

The media plays a major role in the public's perspectives on today's families. For example, the movie *Pleasantville* depicts the most extreme example of traditional families. The children, David and Jennifer, come from a 1990s broken family, but through a magical remote, they are thrust into the world of *Pleasantville* where the mothers are housewives, the fathers make the money, and the children are perfect angels. David and Jennifer turn this world upside down by introducing the norms of their lives in the 1990s that are far different than what the people of Pleasantville are used to. In a classic quote, the mayor of Pleasantville states, "If George doesn't get his dinner, any one of you could be next...it's a question of values" (*Pleasantville*). The plot exemplifies what many people believe families are like. Like in *Pleasantville*, close-minded people who believe that traditional families are the right idea and are the norm for most people are usually the most uneasy about change. The one-sidedness of supporters of traditional families [reveals a lack of] the knowledge of how families actually are in society.

In addition to the movies, many sitcom families are traditional families, which perpetuates the belief that traditional families are the norm in society. Writer Denise Sautters indicates, "*The Adventures of Ozzie and Harriet, The Donna Reed Show,* and *Happy Days* all had something in common—they all represented 'normal' family life. At least in the sense that the husband went to work and the wife spent most of her time in the kitchen." This gives viewers the impression that most families in the country are of the same structure. The real case, however, according to Congresswoman Pat Schroeder, is that "only about 7 percent of all American families fit the Ozzie and Harriet model. Our daily newspapers frequently assert that most children will not grow up in a two-parent family" (qtd. in Wilson 35). With popular television shows depicting families a certain way, the audience receives the impression that the majority of families are of a certain type.

The trend of untraditional families is also evidenced in statistics provided by the government. *The Statistical Abstract of the United States* shows how there has been an increase in single parents living with children. The number of households with men but no spouse raising children has increased from 61,600 to 1,931,000 from 1980 to 2004. Accordingly, the number of females raising children alone has increased from 5,445,000 to 8,221,000 in these twenty-four years. In conjunction with the Census Bureaus data, Tom W. Smith, director of the General Social Survey and the author of "The Emerging 21st-Century American Family," finds that "the most common arrangement in 1972 was married couples with children (45 percent), while in 1998, only 26 percent of households reflected this arrangement" (qtd. in Harms). Over time, families have changed due to a plethora of reasons. With the statistics at hand, it is apparent that most families do not fit the makeup of a traditional family.

Mother May I?

One of the biggest points of disagreement about families is the effectiveness of single mothers with children. Iris Marion Young, professor of political science at the University of Chicago, summarizes former Vice President Dan Quayle's perspectives on single mothers: "Unmarried women with children lie at the source of the 'lawless social anarchy' that sends youth into the streets with torches and guns. Their 'welfare ethos' impedes individual efforts to move ahead in society" (44). Echoing this statement, Barry Glassner, professor of sociology at the University of Southern California, sums up other reports that state, "Newspaper and magazine columnists called illegitimacy 'the smoking gun in a sickening array of pathologies—crime, drug abuse, mental and physical illness, welfare dependency'...and 'an unprecedented national catastrophe'" (94). These points of view from Quayle and other reporters show that some people believe that single mothers are one of the main causes of problems in today's society. They believe that children raised by single mothers are more often the causes of delinquency, violence, and crime. However, these claims are not necessarily the truth.

Defenders of traditional families argue that these new families are harmful to society. Evidence shows that this is not the case. According to Glassner, "Studies that compare single-parent households and two-parent households with similar levels of income, education, and family harmony find few differences in how children turn out" (94). This shows that families without two parents in the home are not any less successful in raising children. Society needs to see that the number of parents in a child's life is not directly related to delinquency. Iris Young notes, "Complex and multiple social causation makes it naïve to think we can conclusively test for clear casual relationship between divorce and children's well being" (45). Young agrees with Glassner in that they both observe that there are few connections between rebellious children and single parents. Statistics that show that there *is* a connection between these two things often ignore the preexisting problems with the family. Young adds, "Many studies of children of divorce fail to compare them to children from 'intact families,' or fail to rule out pre-divorce conditions as causes [of emotional distress]" (45). When studies do not take into account all aspects of a child's life, past and present, it is more difficult to produce an effective and correct study. After seeing the results of these experiments, the public begins to see trends and problems where none exist.

In order to help keep marriages more traditional in today's society, the Bush administration has enacted the Healthy Marriage Initiative. The goal of this legislation is "to increase the number of two-parent families and to reduce out-of-wedlock childbearing" (Rector). According to Robert E. Rector, Senior Research Fellow of Domestic Policy Studies at the Heritage Foundation, and Melissa G. Pardue, Policy Analyst of Domestic Policy Studies at the Heritage Foundation, "The beneficial effects of marriage on individuals and society are beyond reasonable dispute, and there is a broad and growing consensus that government policy should promote rather than discourage healthy marriage." The government is attempting to help society out of its many problems by enacting legislation to cater to the upkeep of traditional families. Therefore, by enacting and enforcing legislation that promotes intact families, the country's problems with poverty and welfare, as well as violence and delinquency, will decrease. Jessica Valenti, Executive Editor of Feministing.com, writes, "This initiative isn't about helping people have healthy marriages, it's about ensuring that they have 'traditional' marriages...the message is clear: men should be the breadwinners, and women should be dependent on them. What Bush wants is happy housewives." With the initiative, the government states that their goal is to promote families so that problems with welfare and poverty decrease. However, what is actually happening is quite different. Valenti goes against the thoughts of Rector and Pardue by pointing out the fact that all the initiative is really doing is putting families into a traditional mold. The conservatives are trying their hardest to put families into a traditional form in order to lessen the amounts of broken families in the country. These acts are not, however, a way to cure society's dilemmas.

Daddy Dearest

The absence of fathers is another one of the main problems cited by people who believe in traditional marriage. Former President Bill Clinton once said, "The single biggest social problem in our society may be the growing absence of fathers from their children's homes, because it contributes to so many other social problems" (qtd. in Glassner 95). In this instance, it appears that having a father in the family is the quickest fix for society's problems today. However, Glassner refutes this argument with, "Men's mere *presence* is apparently adequate to save their children and the nation from ruin...Literature on divorce shows that the main negative impacts on children are conflicts between the parents before the divorce and loss of the father's income afterward rather than absence of the father per se" (96). Glassner shows that the mere absence of the father is not the main cause of problems with separated families. In this case, issues that exist beforehand and the consequences of divorce are more often the causes of problems.

Many others also seem to believe that absentee fathers are one of the main problems in today's society. President of the Institute for American Values, David Blackenhorn, writes, "Fatherlessness is the engine driving our most urgent social problems, from crime to adolescent pregnancy to child sexual abuse to domestic violence against women" (qtd. in Snyder 288). Instead of blaming the decrease in the well being of children on other problems, like poverty, lack of affordable health care, and poor education, Blackenhorn takes the easy route and blames the problems on the lack of fathers. Glassner, however, refutes Blackenhorn's claims with, "If as a group kids from fatherless homes fare less well, this is partly because women have difficulty supporting themselves and their children on what they are paid, and more than half of divorced dads get away with underpayment of child support" (97). With Glassner's testament, it appears that the lack of fathers is not the cause of problems with children. It is the lack of financial support from fathers that is stirring up the most problems. If more laws were created that enforced child support policies, there would most likely be less problems within broken families.

Defenders of traditional families argue that these new families are bad for society. There are many ways in which healthy marriages contribute to the well being of society according to some sources. Dr. Steven E. Rhoads, professor of politics at the University of Virginia, states, "If we care about the future of our kids, we should care about finding the secrets to marriages that last through 'sickness and health,' through 'better and worse.'" He also finds that:

> Marriage is good for society because it gets single men off the
> street...Marriage is good for children because intact families fight crime,
> illegitimacy, depression, drugs, and school failure. And marriage is good for
> individual men and women; married persons are healthier, wealthier, and
> happier than single folks. (5)

With these suggestions, it is portrayed that marriages are the best way for one to achieve happiness and prosperity. However, this evidence fails to take into account any other problems that the family may already have. Young writes:

> <Q1>Families unprotected by wide networks of supportive institutions and
> economic resources are bound to suffer. Ignoring the myriad social
> conditions that affect families only enables the government and the public to
> escape responsibility for investing in the ghettos, building new houses and
> schools, and creating the millions of decent jobs that we need to restore
> millions of people to dignity. (45)

Young, Glassner, and others see beyond what could be coined as the "obvious" problems with fatherless families. When the majority of people are blinded by the stereotypes about families, they do not see the more important issues at hand. Therefore, a large sum of money and manpower are put into reinforcing marriages when it should be pointed in a different direction.

Conclusion

Families have changed in many ways over the decades. The family structure has become less refined and more complicated due to changes in society. People who strive for traditional families argue that these types of families are the best at keeping crime, violence, and poverty under control and under wraps. However, the corruption of families is not the number one cause of these problems like they would like people to believe. Statistics that support these claims often do not take into account the pre-existing conditions of the families at hand. Therefore, new age families can be just as successful and happy as the older, traditional ones. These families may not be a bad mark on society, they just need to be taken into careful consideration by the masses. The media has helped give the impression that traditional families are the most common when, in fact, they are not. All in all, the success of families is held within the family itself. [2,400 words]

Works Cited

Glassner, Barry. *The Culture of Fear.* New York: Basic Books, 1999.

Harms, William. "Marriage Wanes as American Families Enter New Century, University of Chicago Research Shows." *The University of Chicago News Office.* 24 Nov. 1999.

Hite, Shere. "New Family Forms are Emerging." *The Family: Opposing Viewpoints.* Ed. Mary E. Williams. Greenhaven Press: San Diego, 1998. 25-32.

Pleasantville. Dir. Gary Ross. Perf. Tobey Maguire, Reese Witherspoon, William H. Macy, Joan Allen, Jeff Daniels, J.T. Walsh, and Don Knotts. Larger Than Life Productions & New Line Cinema, 1998.

Rector, Robert E. and Melissa G. Pardue. "Understanding the President's Healthy Marriage Initiative." *The Heritage Foundation.* 26 March 2004. 10 April 2006.
    <http://www.heritage.org/Research/Family/bg1741.cfm>.

Rhoads, Steven E. "The Case Against Androgynous Marriage." *The American Enterprise.* 10.5 (1999): 35-39.

Sautters, Denise. "More and More, Gender Roles are a Thing of the Past." *Copley News Service.* 23 Oct. 2005.

Snyder, R. Claire. "Neo-Patriarchy and the Anti-Homosexual Agenda." *Voices of Dissent.* Ed. William F. Grover and Joseph G. Peschek. Pearson Education, Inc: New York, 2006. 282-291.

United States Census Bureau. *Statistical Abstract of the United States.* 4 Jan. 2006. 10 April 2006.
    <http://www.census.gov/prod/www/statistical-abstract.html>.

Valenti, Jessica. "A Good Job is Hard to Find." *AlterNet.* 5 April 2006. 7 April 2006.
    <http://www.alternet.org/story/34161/>.

Wilson, James Q. "Single Parenthood has Harmed the Family." *The Family: Opposing Viewpoints.* Ed. Mary E. Williams. San Diego: Greenhaven Press: 1998. 33-41.

Young, Iris Marion. "Single Parenthood has been Unfairly Stigmatized." *The Family: Opposing Viewpoints.* Ed. Mary E. Williams. San Diego: Greenhaven Press, 1998.

Exercise 26, Sample Literacy Autobiography

Geek Speak

Dustin Fox

Nerd: An unstylish, unattractive, or socially inept person. Especially one slavishly devoted to intellectual or academic pursuits. I am a nerd. Maybe it is not easy to tell by looking at me, but I am. I do not wear glasses or have greasy hair and pimples. I do not wear tapered-leg jeans that are too short and too tight, and I do not own a pocket protector. I am, however, a nerd. Many people have different concepts of what being a nerd means. When I think of what it is, I think of the characters in the movie *Revenge of the Nerds.* Those guys set the standard for being a geek. Everyone has seen a kid who has been labeled a weirdo, nerd, or computer geek. I would say that anyone in one of those categories is a nerd, and I am one of them because I talk like one and act like one, and I am not ashamed.

There are some things about being a nerd that I consider comforting. For one, nerds are good people. Sure, sometimes they dress dorky or talk funny, but what is wrong with that? I feel like being a nerd makes me a part of a club; that is why geeks stick together. It is the kind of positive emotional support that I need in my life. At any time during the day or night, I can go online and at least one of my geeky friends will be awake and willing to play videogames with me. There is nobody like my dorky friends on a night that I am really bored and looking for something to do. Sometimes I get tired of the same old routine of going out to the bar and staring at all the pretty girls who would never take the time to get to know me. So many people are too judgmental; they are too quick to label people and discard them. When someone is aware of his or her own geekiness, it is easier for him or her to be a more accepting individual. That's why I like my friends. We all call each other geeks and nerds too, but we never take it seriously. We are all comfortable talking to and taking ridicule from each other. None of us nerds feels like we are better than anyone else. We may know more about the Internet or computer hardware, but we do not make fun of the people who don't. Having nerds as friends, and being one myself, has really shaped me into the kind of person that I would like to be. I feel like I get along with everyone.

Maybe I am not *quite* as nerdy as the guys in *Revenge of the Nerds,* but I have been called a nerd on several occasions by at least every girl that I am friends with. I talk "normally," but occasionally, a geeky expression will slip out of my mouth when I am excited or not paying attention. I learn these expressions from hanging out with nerdy people or talking to them online. I am a videogame connoisseur. Over the past decade, technology has allowed us to communicate over extremely long distances via the Internet. It is also now possible to play videogames against other people in online real-time. Since the dawn of online gaming, nerds all over the world have been able to collaborate and create interesting new words and sayings with a variety of meanings. It would be hard for someone to spend hours a day online, chatting or playing videogames, and not have some of these words or expressions become a part of their vocabulary. I am consciously aware that, to avoid criticism from other people, I should keep the nerdiness to a minimum while having a conversation with a "normal" person. However, if anyone were to peek over my shoulder at the computer, or listen to me converse with a group of computer geeks, they would immediately see the bright, shining nerd emerge from the body of this normal looking guy. Anyone who has a good friend or sibling who is a die-hard gamer knows exactly what I'm talking about.

Computers are a pain in the ass. Most people do not understand how they work or why they do not work sometimes. I take pride in the fact that I build my own computers and upgrade them on a regular basis. To me, buying a new video card for my computer is comparable to the average guy adding a new performance part to his sports car. Since I have been working on computers for years now, I have developed an extensive technical vocabulary. I could sit and talk all day with another geek about the specs on my new system, but if I were to discuss these things with the average, computer-illiterate person, it would all sound like Chinese to him or her. If I were to say, "My new video card came factory over-clocked an extra twenty megahertz. It has sixteen pipelines and 256 megabits of RAM. I can play Half-Life 2 in 1024x768 resolution with full anti-aliasing and full anisotropic filtering," the translation would be, "My new video card is top-of-the-line. It lets me play the newest games on the highest quality settings." Most of my friends would already understand what that meant because they are just as excited about their computers as I am about mine. However, if someone does not play a lot of computer games and is not knowledgeable on computer hardware, he or she would have no idea what that meant, nor would they care. That was just tech talk. Knowing and understanding those terms does not automatically make someone a computer geek, but actually being excited about a new piece of hardware does.

Girls get excited over a new movie with Brad Pitt or a new music CD. I get excited over those things too; Brad is a good actor, but I *love* videogames. I waited over two years for *Half-Life 2* to be released. I had been excited since I knew of its conception. When it was finally released online at three in the morning last week, I was awake to play it. I stayed up all night playing and did the same all day the next day. My parents bought my brothers and me a Nintendo when I was four years old. I have not played *Super Mario Brothers* in at least ten years, but I can still remember the theme music in my head like I was just playing it yesterday. The entertainment value for videogames is unsurpassed. Videogames require minimal energy, and they are a great way to kill time or put off more important things. I can remember talking about *Mortal Kombat* with my friends in elementary school. I was only in sixth grade, but I could kick people's heads off or rip their hearts out with a special button combination on the controller. It was amazing. Soon, my friends and I were quoting one-liners from the game, like Scorpion's "Get over here!" or Shang Tsung's "Finish him!" at the end of a round. It was the same back then as it is now; if someone had never played the game, he or she would have no idea what our little outbursts were all about. Currently, my roommates and I randomly quote lines from the game *Counter-Strike*, saying, "Fire in the hole!" or "Get outta there, it's gonna blow!" Yes, we are all nerds.

The language of nerds goes much deeper than just quoting something from a videogame. In fact, there have been entirely original words and sayings developed by nerds. They only use these words around other nerds...unless they just want to confuse a normal person. Other words are intentionally misspelled. One example is the word "owned." In a videogame, if one player is beaten brutally by another, it is common to say, "You got owned." Over the years, many times this word has been misspelled on accident. On the keyboard, *P* is located right next to *O;* therefore, sometimes the word is accidentally spelled, "pwned." I do not know whose idea it was to start intentionally misspelling the word, but now everyone is doing it. In fact, it is more common to see someone say, "You got pwned," than to see them spell it correctly. Recently, more variations of "pwned" have surfaced;

pwnt, peezowned, and pawned. Only the biggest nerds ever would know this. I would be lying if I said that I never told someone that I just "pwnt" them.

Although I may not be the classic-type nerd with Coke-bottle glasses and twelve-sided die, I know quite a bit of the ever-growing subculture. However, I am still occasionally caught off-guard in conversations by a word or phrase that I had not previously known. Some of these words have existed for years. One of the words I recently learned was "shazbot." It is a substitute for "shit," that was developed decades ago on the show *Mork & Mindy.* I really wish I would have known about this word growing up. It would have been great to use clever phrases that were substitutes for more profane words in front of my parents. I can imagine walking around as a young boy, feeling clever for saying "shazbot" in front of adults whenever I pleased. I could not get in trouble for saying something that nobody knew the meaning of, right? I tried to make up my own word once—feck. One could imagine what it was supposed to be a substitute for. It only took me saying it one time to my mother to figure out that it was not a clever enough disguise for the real word. I figured I should rely on other people to make up the words for me next time.

Aside from creating words to disguise other inappropriate ones and intentionally misspelling other words, there has been a sublanguage created solely for nerds to use: 1337 5P34K (pronounced "leet speak"). The word "leet" is just a shortened version of the word "elite" which originated from the move *Hackers,* a geek favorite. It still holds the same meaning as the original word as well. The concept of "leet speak" is to use numbers instead of letters, whenever it is possible. Some numbers look like certain letters; an "S" looks like the number five. Some words can be spelled phonetically to conveniently implement the leet speak system. "Dude" can be phonetically spelled D-O-O-D, which can then be converted into leet speak; "d00d." Once people get the hang of it, they can start constructing entire sentences using leet speak and incorporating that with other nerd-enhanced words. "Dude, I just owned you," becomes "d00d, I just pwn3d j00!" I have personally only ever seen people type things like that as a joke; however, I'm sure there are bigger geeks out there that actually take leet speak seriously.

There are many ways to manipulate the rules of spelling and grammar, but they never do a very good job of expressing complex emotions. This is where "emoticons" come into place. Since the advent of online chatting, someone realized that occasionally there is miscommunication. Someone may have been sarcastic while chatting with a friend, but that person became quickly offended. In person, it is easy to tell if people are joking by the look on their faces, or the tone of their voices. Since online chatting is text-based, tone of voice cannot be derived from a message. Some genius figured out that it is possible to simulate facial expressions by using certain characters on a keyboard. A smiley face can be simulated by a colon and right parenthesis. A teeth-barring grin can be simulated by a colon and the letter "D." Pretty much any facial expression can be closely simulated by using a combination of keys. The idea of emoticons has been so widely successful that now, small graphics often replace the keystrokes to form an even better picture of the facial expressions. Even my English teacher uses smiley faces in her e-mails. I guess everyone has a nerdy side—some more than others.

With the exception of emoticons, probably none of the things I described in this essay are actually of any use in "normal" language. However, it is commonplace to incorporate one, if not, many of these things while playing a videogame or talking to another fellow geek. Being a nerd, I know why many of these ideas were established: secrecy. Being a nerd, I know that we have a tendency to feel intimated when someone ridicules us for the way we communicate. Therefore, when I talk with other geeks, it makes me feel normal when they use emoticons, or tell me that it was just "pwned." I know it sounds lame to other people, but everyone is different. I'm glad that I am a nerd and occasionally get to talk like one because it has shaped me into being a more accepting person. I am still critical about others' habits sometimes, but I try not to be. Every time I am about to say something criticizing another person's style, I just stop and think about myself first. I am different in my own way, and everyone else has the right to be, too. Using leet speak, emoticons, and purposely misspelling words may not make someone seem intelligent or cool, but to me, it certainly gives them a colorful personality and makes them more interesting. Some of my best friends are huge dorks, and I do not mind being myself in front of anyone, but I will always relate the best to nerds. [2,283 words]

Joining the English Teacher's Club

Laura Grow

Many people struggle with choosing a career, but I have never wanted to be anything but an English teacher. I grew up in a world of books—I spent a lot of my summer vacation at the library, where I volunteered my time shelving books and helping with the summer reading programs. The secret advantage was that I had first dibs on all the new books. I read every Nancy Drew, Sweet Valley, and Babysitter's Club book before graduating to Stephen King and Dean Koontz. When Pizza Hut held the Book It! reading program, my brother and I both got our free personal pan pizzas every month. My teachers had spelling test charts that held a smiley-face sticker for each perfect score, and my line was always straight smileys. My high school did not have the best English program, but I took in Shakespeare, Steinbeck, and Chaucer with enthusiasm. Although I don't have a creative bent, writing was never a problem, and I never earned less than an A on my essays. English was my passion, and teaching was more than just a good outlet for it; teaching was in my blood. From subjecting my brother to hours of playing school to helping classmates with difficult concepts to tutoring younger children, I was never more at ease than when I was in that role. So I entered college a great deal more settled than most freshmen do, eager to get on with my education so I could be on the other side of the desk. Little did anyone know, however, that I harbored a secret, one that I was sure would get me banned from the English Teacher Club for life should it get out: I hated poetry.

I always loved the ambiguity of studying novels and short stories, the exploration of layers of meaning. But for some reason, poetry never had the same effect on me. I understood the poetic conventions—metaphor, allusion, alliteration, and all the others— but I found the actual poems dense and confusing, and I utterly lacked the patience to conduct the multiple readings necessary to understand them. I considered myself fortunate not to have been exposed to a lot of poetry in high school, but the few instances I was assigned it were the only times I felt lost in an English classroom. I had a sense, however, that any English teacher worth his or her salt was able to quote Wordsworth, Blake, or Milton upon request, attended poetry readings in dark, smoky bars, and kept a copy of *Leaves of Grass* handy at all times for pleasure reading, so I kept my distaste for poetry safely closeted.

It was with much trepidation, therefore, that I anticipated the poetry component of my introductory literature course during my first year of college. The course was divided into short story, drama, and poetry units, with an analytical paper required in each of the genres. "The Bride Comes to Yellow Sky" and *Hamlet* were no problem, enjoyable even, but I was at a loss for a poem to explicate. English 102 was a required class, so most students muddled through it with a decided lack of enthusiasm, but I was an English major and I felt that way. I was a fraud! On a whim, I approached my teacher, Mrs. Luther, with an idea. Rather than examining a conventional poem, she allowed me to analyze song lyrics for my essay, a decision that opened the door to poetry to me at last.

*   *   *

I was a Johnny-come-lately to the music scene. In elementary school, when all my little friends were buying New Kids on the Block, Tiffany, and Debbie Gibson tapes, I could not have cared less. In middle school, I had a Mariah Carey tape or two, and a great affection, inherited from my father, for the Beach Boys, but I was no lover of music. In retrospect, I can see that one of the main reasons was that popular music at the time did not offer anything that appealed to what really makes me tick. I love language—word play, metaphor, imagery, story-telling—and the pop music of the late '80s had all the lyrical complexity of a greeting card.

In 1992, although I only nominally appreciated music, I was nonetheless mesmerized by the Columbia House mail-order music service advertisement in my YM magazine. Ten free tapes sounded like a good deal to me, so I made my selections and eagerly awaited their arrival. When the box finally came, I ripped it open and took inventory

145

of my new music collection: Boyz II Men, Paula Abdul, C + C Music Factory, Wilson Phillips, more Mariah Carey, Pearl Jam. Wait, Pearl Jam? One of those things was not like the others. Columbia House had made a mistake and sent me the wrong selection; I didn't even know what Pearl Jam was. Irritated but nevertheless curious to find out just what this oddly-named band was all about, I opened the cellophane and played the tape. Although it sounds overly dramatic, to state anything less would be untruthful: Columbia House's error was about to change my life.

I had never heard anything like it. A thumping bass line led the way into screaming electric guitar, all overlaid with Eddie Vedder's deep, powerful vocals. It was certainly a far cry from the bubblegum pop to which I was accustomed. It took less than one song and I was hooked. Most of the other tapes that came that day were never even played. I fell in love with Pearl Jam and with rock and roll, and I never looked back.

Just as important as the music that moved me were Vedder's lyrics. For the first time, I was hearing songs that expressed emotions in something more than just rhyme. I had always enjoyed a good love song, even ones about love gone wrong. At one time Mariah Carey's "Someday" had topped my list. It is a catchy tune, but not exactly a masterpiece of lyrical poetics. Eddie Vedder, however, was a poet. The first time I heard Pearl Jam's "Black," a searing song about lost love full of rich imagery and metaphor, I knew I would never enjoy Mariah Carey again. Vedder expressed himself eloquently, and when paired with the genius musicianship of his band mates, Pearl Jam's album was more than just an auditory experience for me; I felt the music.

Another characteristic that set Pearl Jam's music apart from the vapid pop was that their songs were not just love songs. Vedder wrote about social issues of homelessness, child abuse, and choice; for the first time, I realized that music could really be *about* something. I knew language had certainly influenced my life and challenged my perspectives, and there was something very appealing to me in the notion of songs with a message. I became a music nut. The Seattle grunge scene was my first love: Pearl Jam above all others, Alice in Chains, Soundgarden, and to a lesser degree, Nirvana. As rock music experienced a renaissance through the early and mid-'90s, so did I. I embraced Marilyn Manson, Metallica, Live, The Cranberries, Liz Phair, Sarah McLachlan, Tori Amos. Musically, there was no real tie that bound my favorite artists together; they range from heavy metal to a woman and her piano. The common thread that endeared them all to me was (and is) that they all have a gift with words, a way of expressing their pain, joy, dreams, and concerns that transcends the mundane.

*   *   *

In spite of the fact that I respected the lyrical integrity of the songs I loved, I always considered them different from the "legitimate" poetry we studied in school. That all changed, however, the day that Mrs. Luther gave me permission to analyze a song's lyrics.

With her stamp of approval to validate my opinion about music, I realized that maybe I did not dislike poetry; maybe I just hadn't given certain types of poetry a chance. The more I considered my love of music in contrast to my disdain for poems, the more I realized that my aversion was more a product of my own mental block than any inherently confusing quality about poetry. I understood the metaphor and imagery of song lyrics and appreciated their alliteration, assonance, and other word play; I relished in the complexity of music because I gave it a chance. Perhaps that is an understatement—I more than gave it a chance. I awaited the release of every new Pearl Jam album with the excitement of a child on Christmas morning, and when they were finally mine, I listened to them endlessly, memorizing every chord change and vocal intonation. To this day, I do not need crib sheets to reproduce the lyrics of my favorite songs; they are part of the fabric of who I am. Once an English professor gave me permission to consider those songs poetry, I finally understood that if I approached canonical poetry with the same openness and passion that I devoted to my favorite lyrics, I would likely develop at minimum an appreciation for poetry that would help me feel less fraudulent as an English major.

My explication of Pearl Jam's "Rearviewmirror" was an A paper. I entered my American literature class the following semester with a renewed attitude, and I opened myself up to Longfellow, Poe, Dickinson, and Whitman. I can't say that I developed a love for all of them that parallels my love of Eddie Vedder or Tori Amos, but Dickinson and Poe certainly come close. As I continued my education, I was exposed to other poets who also won me over, among them Keats, Donne, and Plath. I completed my English degree successfully, and although I will never be the type of teacher who can recite a poem on cue, I am free of the closeted loathing of poetry that haunted my earlier years.

In an interesting coincidence, when I finally got to teach a literature course for the first time, it was English 102 at the same community college I had attended several years earlier. I would be lying if I said that I was not nervous about beginning the requisite poetry unit; I was afraid I wouldn't be as enthusiastic about it as I had been about short stories and Shakespeare, and that it would affect my students' attitudes. After some initial contemplation about how to introduce the unit, I realized the answer was not in the enormous literature anthology I was staring at; it was sitting on my very full CD rack. Out came the Tori Amos, Tool, Nickelback, Type O Negative, and of course Pearl Jam. We listened to the songs, analyzed the lyrics, and talked about the idea that poetry is not merely confined to literature books. I know my lessons did not catch all my students in the thrall of poetry, but from their feedback both in person and on the class evaluations, I know that some of them were reached. I have Eddie Vedder and Mary Luther to thank for the fact that I didn't turn out to be a fraud of an English teacher after all. [2,040 words]